The Horse in Winter

'Practical advice and lots of labour- and time-saving tips on the difficulties of caring for horses and ponies in winter.' *Pony*

'Many years' experience have been condensed into this valuable volume.' *Yorkshire Post*

Susan McBane began riding at the age of four and has many years' experience of riding and looking after her own and other people's horses and ponies in varying circumstances.

She is Secretary of the Equine Behaviour Study Circle and has been an equestrian writer for over twenty years, writing for many major publications in Great Britain and abroad. She founded *Equi* in 1980 and edited it for five years.

The Horse in Winter

HIS MANAGEMENT AND WORK

Susan McBane

THE KINGSWOOD PRESS

First published in Great Britain 1988
by Methuen London
Reprinted 1991
First paperback edition published 1991
by The Kingswood Press, an imprint of Methuen London
Michelin House, 81 Fulham Road, London SW3 6RB

Copyright © 1988 Susan McBane
A CIP catalogue record for this book
is available from the British Library

ISBN 0 413 18080 8 (hardback)
ISBN 0 413 66040 0 (paperback)

Printed in England by Clays Ltd, St Ives plc

Contents

In memory of Johnny, who would jump anything, but not with a rider!

List of Illustrations

Preface and Acknowledgements

Of all the seasons of the year, winter is the hardest and most unpleasant for horse owners and managers and the one in which horses and ponies can suffer most due to particular health, management and work-related difficulties. Many horses are at the extreme ends of management systems: they are either stabled all the time and, often because they belong to working owners who, for various reasons, do not exercise them enough, spend months bored and frustrated, or they are turned out and suffering from exposure and cold, which is possible in even a mild winter. Probably the only comparable time of year in terms of extreme discomfort for the horse is high summer, when insect attacks make the lives of unprotected horses a misery.

Whether animals are working or resting, kept indoors or out, winter brings unique and often severe problems encountered at no other time and, because of this, demands specialised knowledge and techniques which test to the full the competence and commitment of those responsible for looking after them.

This book aims to show that, with some thought and preparation, it *is* possible, using realistic methods and quite ordinary facilities, to bring a horse or pony through even a hard winter in a happy frame of mind and healthy physical condition – and without too much stress on his human connections!

The book is not a general horse-care manual containing the sort of information found in every such book, and it does assume a basic knowledge and some experience of horse management. It concentrates specifically on winter topics and relates management practices to winter conditions. For instance, it does not give a full treatment of every aspect of feeding horses as it is assumed that readers will know the basics. It does, though, pick out aspects of feeding which relate specially to winter. In this way, I hope it will be of especial value to owners with the responsibility of looking after a horse during a most testing time of year.

For their help with various aspects of this book I should like to thank Janet Eley BVSc, MRCVS, Gillian McCarthy BSc (Hons) and also Frances Phillips, Diane Hall and Margot Tiffany.

1 Climate and Weather

The climatic zones of the earth present special tests of survival to those creatures living in them. From the bitter cold and dryness of the poles, which merge into the vast, wind-whipped tundras, to the temperate zones, semi-tropical and tropical regions, each climatic area tends to create its own specific community of plants, animals and other life-forms which are best fitted to survive in it. Those organisms which are less well suited to a certain environment tend not to thrive (without the artificial help of man). They live shorter lives, breed fewer descendants and eventually die out, leaving the better suited organisms to live and flourish. It is a case of evolutionary 'horses for courses'.

Some creatures, notably the larger land mammals (such as man and the horse) and birds, are able to wander about not only their climatic zone but the entire planet, and, while remaining members of their own species, diverge into specific types over evolutionary time (which, of course, is many millions of years) with physical features enabling them to survive best in a particular area. Some habitually migrate from one zone to another, birds being a prime example of this; others manage to overcome the extremes of the region in which they seem to prefer to stay by such techniques as hibernation, which enables them to live in a state of 'suspended animation' through conditions they would normally find intolerable.

Horses, when they were wild, did not migrate from one climatic zone to another for, for example, breeding purposes, but they were able to migrate from one feeding area to another, which often entailed treks of many hundreds of miles. A present-day example of this is the migration of the zebras, who accompany the wildebeeste in their twice-yearly odyssey up and down Africa.

Nor do horses hibernate, but the races within the species have developed various physical features to enable them to withstand particular climatic conditions. Some behavioural adaptations also occur, such as pawing down through snow to get at grass or reaching up to trees to browse leaves.

Experts in all fields are known to differ in their professional opinions; even when there are facts on which to base those opinions, an individual's interpretation of those facts often results in an opinion at variance with those of colleagues. As regards the development of physical characteristics of the different races of horses, the most commonly held view among zoologists and evolutionists is that before the domestication of the horse (which – again according to opinion – seems to have been roughly between four and five thousand years ago) there existed four basic horse types – a northern horse and northern pony and a southern horse and southern pony. Although the division between horse and pony is often still today decided by height (anything under 15 hands high being generally regarded as a pony), and was so decided by the zoologists and evolutionists, height is less important than other physical characteristics when assessing an animal's ability to survive in a given environment.

The northern types, height apart, had characteristics which distinguished them clearly from their southern relatives. For a start, they grew longer, thicker coats in winter, often with a 'second' coat or soft underlayer for extra insulation. Their ribcages were usually rounded, or 'well sprung' in horsey terminology, as animals so built are able to retain body heat more effectively than more 'slab-sided' animals. The coat, particularly in winter, grew long, coarse 'cat' or guard hairs to assist drainage of water from the body, particularly under the jaw, on the sides and the lower extremities of the legs. The mane and tail hair was coarser and more luxuriant than in the southern races, again aimed at keeping more insulating air close to the body, and the skull tended to be larger and heavier, often tending towards a Roman nose, to provide bigger air passages for the warming of the cold air before it reached the lungs. The nostrils themselves were more slit-like to prevent excessive heat loss from the thin mucous membrane-covered tissue inside. The carriage of the tail was also low, and it was lower set, again, to prevent heat loss from the thinner skin between the buttocks and hind legs. And the skin itself was thicker in the northern equidae than the southern, for added protection against cold rain and wind and to help retain heat. Some experts also say that northern group animals can constrict the blood capillaries in the skin more effectively than can the southern group ones, to keep heat-filled blood deeper inside the body.

As might be expected, the southern horses and ponies had characteristics opposite to those described above. Their heads were smaller, often with a straight or even 'dished', concave face and larger, more mobile nostrils. Their coats both in winter and summer were shorter and finer to facilitate heat loss in summer and protect against the chill experienced even in a warmer winter. Many southern types were not so rounded in the body (as evidenced in many Thoroughbreds and similar breeds today which, despite having a good deal of oriental ancestry, are also descended from northern strains), and their mane, tail and leg hair (where it exists at all) is much finer. Their tail carriages, particularly in Arab-type horses, are higher, and actually set higher in most cases, to allow heat to escape from the body, and the skin is usually thinner for the same reason. Southern-type animals often tend to sweat more, and more easily, than their northern counterparts, the sweat playing an essential role in temperature control.

From a general assessment of these major differences in physique, it is obvious that the type of animal best fitted to survive through winter with little if any help from man (natural resources of food, water and shelter being sufficient) is the northern type. British native ponies are so called because they have been here since the end of the last Ice Age and are perfectly fitted to our climate.

Apart from the British and Irish native breeds, there are many Russian breeds with the same basic characteristics, and Scandinavian breeds such as the Norwegian Fjord Pony, the Icelandic Pony and the Austrian Haflinger.

Larger breeds, such as all the heavy horse breeds, Cleveland Bays and suchlike also have, within their racial or breed characteristics, the physique to withstand a temperate zone or sub-arctic winter given reasonable conditions of shelter, food and water.

All the northern types have evolved with physical characteristics to prevent excessive heat loss and, therefore, to use as little energy and food as possible. Thus apart from being cheaper to keep in our climate they are often more practical. However, many southern-type animals do winter well in northern climes.

Horses and ponies, like other animals and humans, adapt to some extent as individuals to changes in climate and conditions, not only during the natural yearly cycle of the seasons but in moves from one area to another and even one hemisphere to another. They can tolerate greater extremes of temperature than humans and can be 'hardened up' or 'softened up' similarly. Just as a human being used to centrally heated conditions can really feel the cold, despite other sources of heat, when that heating breaks down or when moving from, say, a centrally heated home to one that is not, horses, too, can have their individual tolerance changed by conditioning.

I once bought an Anglo-Arab colt from East Anglia, well known for its bitter winter (by British standards) and cold east winds straight from Russia and Scandinavia. He had lived out for three winters with his Thoroughbred dam when I bought him and, in fact, was running out with her and his sister in deep snow when I made the trip to see him during the severe (for Britain) winter of 1962–3, and very well they all looked, too.

In his new home with me at a livery stable, he was kept on the combined system. Three years later, after a respiratory illness had left him with sensitive lungs, I tried, on veterinary advice, to return him to living out permanently, but he had become used to being stabled at nights and could not stand being permanently out as autumn progressed into winter. I was told at the time that it can take a horse two years or even more to readjust but the horse was so miserable that I was not prepared to make him put up with it and carried on stabling him at night.

Other horses I have known well have readapted better but not all equally. It is well known that when horses are exported from Great Britain to Australia they very often persist in growing their winter coat in the Australian summer for two years or more, and that some individuals adapt and acclimatise better than others. There is also a good deal of variety within breeds. For example, some Thoroughbreds are extremely thin-skinned and sensitive while others are quite tough and winter out in snow and cold winds with natural shelter such as a spinney and good hedges plus good feeding, seeming quite happy and well.

Perhaps of all the seasons of the year, winter is the one where horse owners and managers must really study each horse closely as an individual if intending to keep the animals mainly out, to see if they genuinely can withstand the conditions, with or without human help.

Horses, like other creatures, have inner 'biological rhythms' which are controlled by the seasons. Even if we are not all 'ruled by the moon' – and no one seems certain yet whether we actually are or not – what *is* known is that biological rhythms are controlled by light, temperature and food intake. Horses' minds and, particularly, their bodies are controlled by and respond to these three factors. Provided nothing drastic, like being exported to a different climatic zone, happens to the horse, the seasonal changes it goes through follow a regular yearly pattern and are fairly predictable.

In mid-winter, the horse is wearing his winter coat. Even if it has been clipped off he has still grown it. Neither mares nor stallions are thinking of breeding and, in natural conditions, their time and attention is taken up finding what food and water they can and sheltering from the elements. Survival is paramount now.

But after the shortest day of the year on 21 December (in the northern hemisphere) subtle changes occur in the horse's body. Although the worst of the winter weather may not yet have arrived, the days start to get longer, which means that the horse is subjected to increasing amounts of daylight. Very gradually, this change registers in the horse's brain. The pineal gland in the brain receives messages along the optic nerves from the eyes (which have sensed the increasing daylight) and sends out chemical messages by means of substances called hormones to 'instruct' or programme the body to start preparing for spring. The pituitary gland gives out follicle-stimulating hormone and luteinising hormone (FSH and LH) which control the sexual cycle in mares, and interstitial cell stimulating hormone (ICSH), which causes the production of the male sex hormone testosterone. As the days lengthen, the sex hormones increase, which is why horses are naturally most sexually active when the days are at their longest and the light most intense.

The pituitary also influences the production of the thyroid gland, which in turn influences hair growth and casting. The horse obviously needs a thinner coat in summer than in winter, so the signal goes out to start casting the winter coat. This happens very gradually, and most owners only notice a significant amount of hair loss in late winter. The summer coat is often not fully set until May, or even later. It is noticeable that 'late' foals (those born later in the year) often lose their winter coat later than early foals, and get it back again later, too.

The sexual activity and summer coat production coincide with the germination of seed and the growth of grass, which are also influenced by light and warmth, so that at the time when foals are born in nature the grass is at its most nutritious.

Still in what we call high summer, the days are noticeably shortening. By August, despite the temperature and climate, most horses have already started to cast their summer coats, sexual activity is waning and grass is less protein-rich than in spring. And so the cycle begins again.

In fact, the horse's entire metabolism changes gradually all the time. There is an old saying that a horse is never at his best when casting, and this often seems to be true. Some horses seem to be 'winter horses', being at their most zestful then, while others do best, and work best, in summer.

Coat growth is significantly controlled by temperature, and, as detailed in Chapter 5, it is quite possible artificially to control it to our own ends whatever the amount of light available.

Horses out in winter, particularly those in restricted domestic situations such as small paddocks, with insufficient shelter and possibly erratic or insufficient feeding, are under increasing stress as winter progresses. The worst time for them is the last half of winter – January, February and March. April, sadly, often sees many deaths as animals come to the end of their tether. They have endured long months of cold, probably wet and wind in Britain, usually at least some snow and ice and maybe poor food supplies, yet despite lengthening days the grass is not really coming through yet except in the very south of the country, and because of decreased body condition, even if the temperature is warming up a little, they still feel the cold badly.

Even good feeding is not enough on its own to ensure an animal's survival through the winter; shelter and a skin and coat in good condition are also needed. Animals can also die of hypothermia, and it is quite possible for an animal to become hypothermic without being thin.

Just as it is nature's way gradually to produce by evolution animals and plants best fitted to a particular environment, it is also her way to ensure that only the best fitted survive to spring, to breed and pass on those 'suitable' genes to offspring who, in turn, will be likely to survive. By killing off those less well suited to a particular environment before they get chance to leave offspring, nature hones to a fine edge the characteristics of the creatures involved. By the time the days are long, the air is warm and the grass at its best, foals and other young animals are being born, to give them the best possible start in a rigorous life.

Racing Thoroughbreds, at least flat racers, do not have these natural advantages. In the early days of the breed's existence, the official birthday of all Thoroughbreds was 1 May. It was fairly soon changed to 1 January in an effort to achieve earlier maturity, so that, let us face it, greedy humans could get the youngsters on to the racecourse and winning money or proving themselves as potential high-class breeding stock as soon as possible. Other performance breeds also now designate this artificial birth date for their registered animals.

The result is that foals, often of the thin-skinned Thoroughbred type and its descendants and not the tougher, hardy northern type, are born in mid-winter, with at least two and probably three months of bitterly cold and/or wet weather to contend with. Because such conditions would kill them if they were left out, it is necessary to house them (which costs money), feed them artificially (which costs money), employ more staff to carry out the increased labour involved (which costs money) and use artificial lighting and sometimes heating in the running of the studs where they are born (which costs money). However, the value of these animals makes the increased initial costs well worthwhile in some cases, so owners, breeders and trainers put up with the costs of artificially combating winter for the usually slim chance of producing a highly valuable world-beater.

Many experts, both veterinary surgeons and professional breeders and trainers, would like a return to more natural conditions, not least because the majority of the animals born will never repay their costs but also because they appreciate that in the long run nature does know best, and the animals would get off to a better start in life if allowed to breed according to nature's cycles. However, until there are more breeders, trainers and potential owners who are prepared to allow the horse to mature more naturally and to begin working a year or more later than at present, and to continue his or her career as a mature animal (in the case of Thoroughbreds), so really proving his or her capabilities and giving future breeders a true picture of the stock being produced, it seems that the situation will not change. There are many people in horse breeding (all breeds, it seems) who are willing to expend money to sustain the artificial system and similarly to expend those animals not able to fit in with that system.

If you *are* in the business of producing horses whose birthdays are officially 1 January you will need to know how best to get mares and stallions to become sexually active, and the mares cycling regularly, by the middle of February (in the northern hemisphere) when the stud season starts. Provided you have basic facilities such as electric light, stabling and the money to provide clothing and food, you will probably have no problem, and a little help from your veterinary surgeon, if needed, will put the lid on it, particularly with 'problem' mares.

The first tactic is to expose the horses (mares *and* stallions, for the latter are influenced by the same factors) to increasing amounts of daylight around the time of the winter solstice (shortest day) or just before. This is usually done by leaving the lights on in the stables for longer and longer periods of time until the horses are exposed to 16 hours out of 24 of light, either natural daylight or a mixture of daylight and electric light.

When the horses are brought in for the evening, the lights are usually left on till midnight to achieve this but it has been found that exposing them to just one hour of artificial light between 2 a.m. and 3 a.m. has the same effect. This can be done by fitting a timer switch to the lighting system, which is easily done by a competent electrician and is not expensive. You will also save money by not leaving the lights on for unnecessary extra hours.

The second tactic is to keep the horses warm. Obviously they have to be exercised, usually by turning out, so New Zealand rugs can be used, or exercise sheets for stallions being walked or barren mares being ridden. Rugs can be used in the stables at night. Some studs heat stables artificially but others believe that this increases stuffiness and encourages respiratory disorders, so this is a matter for individual choice.

The third thing to do is to make sure the horses are in good bodily condition. They must be neither too thin nor gross. Again, the eye of the master comes in here. Whoever is in charge of feeding must be able to judge when an individual horse is in just the right condition for conception to be more likely.

Fourthly, linked with condition is an adequate balanced diet to provide all the nutrients necessary for the metabolism to work at its best, to bring the animals into good condition and sexual activity and encourage good health and fertility.

The final factor is fitness. We hear a good deal about stallions needing to be fit for their arduous stud duties, and this is true, but this does not mean galloping/racing fit. When horses go to stud out of training, or straight from any high-level physical activity, they often need a period to let down, relax and soften up a little before they are in breeding condition. Many barren mares are sent to stud without any effort to get them even moderately fit, whereas gentle exercise such as an hour a day hacking would do them nothing but good, assuming they can be ridden.

As far as stallion fitness goes, in Britain and Ireland it is most unusual for Thoroughbred stallions to be ridden, yet this is the only really practical way to get them reasonably fit. We see stallion men walking them in hand for miles and hours daily, which is certainly better than nothing, but from a fitness point of view barely scratches the surface. Sometimes they are lunged as well, and most are allowed to stretch their legs in a paddock, but the system employed on the continent of Europe and in some studs in other countries where competent riders are employed specially to ride the stallions, relieves the stallion men of a very time-consuming and not very effective task and gets the job done so much better. This continuing to be ridden also makes difficult stallions easier to handle, and it does not add to the stud's wage bill as fewer stallion men can be employed.

Again, the stallions do not need to be as fit as when they were at the peak of their athletic careers, but reasonable fitness is certainly an advantage to the production of healthy sperm, general well-being and, therefore, adequate sex drive.

The above factors all need attention during the winter if breeding stock are to be given the best chance to be productive. Many would, of course, produce foals anyway, but fertility rates in many breeds, particularly the Thoroughbred, leave a lot to be desired, so surely anything we can do to improve them must be all to the good, particularly when one considers the high cost involved in keeping and breeding horses. A barren year for a small-time mare owner can be financially disastrous, and for the stallion owner high fertility figures can only enhance his horse's reputation.

If the above methods do not result in early sexual activity and mares show no sign of coming into season, veterinary surgeons can help significantly.

If a mare has shown no signs at all of coming into season (and some do come into season without showing), it has to be determined whether she is not cycling at all (known as anoestrus) or between seasons (dioestrus). The veterinary surgeon can take a blood sample to determine the level of progesterone (a hormone) circulating, which will tell him or her whether the mare is dioestrus or anoestrus. Most vets would wish to do this about the beginning of February, bearing in mind that the stud season starts about the middle of that month.

A dioestrus mare would subsequently be given a prostaglandin injection which would bring her into season. With an anoestrus mare, once the system of exposing her to extra light has been followed for fifty days, a feed supplement called Regumate, consisting of the drug allyl trenbolone, is given for ten days. After this, another blood sample can be taken to determine whether the mare is now dioestrus or still anoestrus. If she is dioestrus she can then be given a prostaglandin injection and should ovulate seven days later.

Another method is to insert an IUD (intra-uterine device) to stimulate her to come into season.

Obviously, all these methods are carried out by a veterinary surgeon, but are usually very successful in bringing a mare into season, ensuring ovulation and, hopefully, conception.

Other reasons for a mare not conceiving, apart from problems with the stallion, are usually infection or malconformation of her breeding organs. Again, both these factors are the domain of the veterinary surgeon.

The actual weather during the winter can influence breeding stock, of course, as well as other animals. If the weather is really harsh, all our efforts to kid the horses into thinking it is spring may be less effective than in a milder winter and, after being 'artificially induced' to come into season, the mare could be covered, not conceive or resorb the foetus and become anoestrus again. In some mild winters, the grass keeps growing slowly throughout, although its nutrient content will not be really significant till spring. However, it will certainly have some effect on the animals' mental and physical conceptions of the season.

It is particularly frustrating when, having had a very mild winter up to, say, the end of January, we get a sudden hard frost with snow, ice and bitter winds in February, March and maybe even April, putting the animals (and the grass) right back into winter mode just when we were hoping to move into an early spring!

Horses can stand quite intense cold if the weather is dry and still; it is wind and wet, particularly combined, which affect them badly if exposed, despite good feeding. Wind and wet intensify the effect of the cold and can seriously chill animals. Good feeding alone is not enough to counteract these effects.

Youngstock, particularly weanlings experiencing their first winter, need special care if they are not to suffer from exposure and become stunted. Growth hampered during the first year of life is never made up later, so those animals will never attain their full potential development or physical ability.

Because most domestic situations, consisting as they usually do of railed or wire-fenced paddocks, do not provide enough shelter, it is usually best to bring even native bred animals in at night during their first winter. True, a winter on Dartmoor, the Welsh Hills or the Cumbrian Fells may seem excessively harsh to us, but animals living wild do know where to go to find their own shelter, which is often very effective. In a domestic paddock perhaps all they have is a single hedge, maybe not even on the windward side of the field.

Another point to bear in mind is that animals living wild,

even under the ultimate supervision of man, are subject to natural selection after a fashion – the weakest (usually the young, sick and old) may well not survive till spring. Only the hardiest youngsters survive in wild and feral conditions, and this is not a policy most breeders, even of native stock, wish to adopt with their animals, unless they are breeding them naturally simply for the meat market, as some native pony breeders do.

If we have the interests of the animals themselves at heart, bringing them in at night, or providing truly adequate shelter out of doors, is essential.

Weanlings of 'performance' breeds, usually containing a good deal of Thoroughbred or Arab blood and their crosses, should not be expected to do well without proper shelter; most breeders of this type of animal would certainly stable or yard them at night, even if their turn-out facilities offer good shelter. This regular bringing in also helps the handlers to keep a keen eye on them, facilitates handling, basic lessons in stable manners and adequate feeding in a non-competitive situation. Even when they are fed together, at least someone is able to note if a particular individual is not getting its share and can take steps to correct that.

Weanlings should be established on an adequate, balanced ration (with the help of a vet or nutritionist) *before* weaning. Weaning as carried out in most commercial western studs is usually too sudden and too soon, and many youngsters suffer greatly at this time, causing considerable loss of condition at a time (coming into winter and during fast growth) when they can least afford it. If they are used to 'man-made' food as opposed to, or rather in addition to, their natural foods of mother's milk plus grass, they will recover that much quicker and their weight loss should be minimal.

For horse foals, it is generally felt that for the first year of life they should consume 1 lb of concentrates per day for every month of life, so at weaning, which usually takes place about six months of age, they should be readily eating about 6 lbs of concentrates daily, plus what hay they want.

A more precise calculation is to feed according to body-weight; up to 18 months of age, 2·5 per cent to 3 per cent of the animal's weight should be fed, including concentrates and hay.

Unless you have access to a weighbridge, the simplest way to learn your animal's weight is to buy a special measuring tape which is marked with measurements (taken round the girth) and gives the amount of feed recommended daily. A suitable tape is Equitape, available from the Equine Management Consultancy Service, 20 Victoria Road, Bulwark, Chepstow, Gwent NP6 5QN. Although this is intended for mature animals, it does give you a fair idea of your youngster's weight, and you will be able to tell whether or not it is making even weight gains (as it should) while growing. The EMCS also gives professional advice on feeding and all matters relating to horse and pony management.

As youngsters' digestive systems have not yet developed to cope with large amounts of hay, the ratio should be about two-thirds concentrates to one-third hay. Of course, when grass is available, the whole matter becomes more complicated, and again the advice of a vet or nutritionist should be sought. By the time spring grass comes through, however, owners should have a fair idea of the individual foals' idiosyncracies as regards feed, i.e. whether they are good or poor doers, which should help to avoid the consequences of serious blunders.

Although snow covers up the ground, and therefore whatever grass there is, horses do not seem to mind it too much. Deep snow, however, does prevent them from moving about sufficiently. They tend to make tracks to and from shelter, feeding and watering areas and keep to them, and some animals have the instinct to paw down through snow to get at what greenery remains. Many animals, particularly when first turned out into snow, frolic and play about just like other young animals and children, not to mention roll in it.

Although basically frozen water, snow does not wet and chill animals like rain does. Particularly in native-bred animals with a thick insulating coat, the snow can often be seen lying in a white layer over their backs, but if you push your fingers through the coat underneath, they are as warm as toast. It is when the snow melts (as it does sooner in finer-coated animals) and soaks the coat that problems can occur (see next chapter).

Frozen, crusty snow can also cut and scratch the legs and nose, creating inlets for bacteria and resulting in infected wounds, and this must be watched for in susceptible animals. However, I feel that we in Britain often keep our horses in too much in snow, and could well take a leaf out of other countries' books, particularly the Americans', and let our horses use their common sense about exercising themselves in snow. Ailments caused by turning animals out seem rarer, in my experience, than those caused by keeping them in!

Damp conditions are much more unpleasant for horses and humans alike than cold, dry ones, snow or no snow. The damp seems to get everywhere and intensify the low temperature. Moisture-laden air makes breathing less effective and harder work, and the normal resilient, air-containing winter coat is easily bedraggled and flattened, and therefore less insulating, in damp conditions, so horses feel the cold more. This is exacerbated by the fact that air is a poor conductor of heat whereas water is a good one. A damp atmosphere conducts heat easily away from the body, which feels colder quicker than in a dry atmosphere.

Because body resources are used partly to keep up the body's temperature, more energy is needed to keep warm on a cold, damp day than on a dry day with the same air temperature. Consistent exposure to damp may not itself cause diseases but it can, by depleting available energy resources, make a horse more prone to infections by lowering its resistance.

Probably in winter more than at any other time, particularly if we have horses to look after, we want to know what the weather is going to do. Here in Britain, where the weather is a constant topic of conversation, we often seem to have a climate which does not usually go to extremes but which is at best unpredictable and unstable. An American visitor once said to me: 'I've never visited any other country and had spring, summer, autumn and winter all in one day.' He had a point!

Apart from paying close attention to the weather forecast on the radio and television (which often seems to be as unreliable as our weather!), it is a good idea to do a little amateur study of the weather, a detailed but easy-to-understand book, I have found, being *Beginner's Guide to Weather Forecasting* by Stanley Wells. A reliable barometer is helpful as are periodic conversations with someone who works outside such as a farmer or a brick-layer, whose work is closely controlled by the weather.

I always used to laugh when my grandmother said she could tell when it was going to freeze because her bunions played up, but she was usually right.

Cloud formations can be tricky to learn, especially in winter when the sky seems to be one big cloud, but simple things can help, like learning that a clear evening with a ring round the moon means frost and that old poem:

> Red at night, shepherd's delight.
> Red in the morning, shepherd's warning.

If we have some idea of what to expect, at least we can prepare by, say, putting an extra blanket on the horse that night or, if the wind is going to be blowing right into the boxes, just leaving the windows open for ventilation but shutting the doors as an exception.

Preparation in other areas, too, helps to prevent being caught unawares. Seasonal jobs for autumn which could help to avoid a major or minor catastrophe include checking the stability of the field shelter and the state of the roof, clearing out and repairing the stable guttering ready for heavy rains, ensuring that all water pipes are properly lagged with old sacks or whatever is available, to avoid freezing up, getting clipper blades sharpened in plenty of time (ideally in the spring!), ensuring that your supply of rugs and blankets is adequate and that everything is in good repair and clean (again, ideally this should be done in spring), checking and having the drains cleaned out to prevent winter flooding, getting a supply of barrier cream or other protective substance if you have a horse prone to mud fever, discussing well in advance with your farrier about frost nails and studs if you need to work your horse as opposed to turning him out, and building up a supply of old cooking fat from the kitchen to grease his soles with in snowy weather.

Spring jobs, apart from the clipper blades and rugs already mentioned, include spring-cleaning and thoroughly disinfecting boxes (a hired steam or pressure cleaner makes light work of this), clearing out deep litter bedding and rounding up whatever hay you can find as supplies begin to run short (methods of overcoming a hay shortage are discussed in Chapter 4).

2 Body Temperature and its Importance

The creatures living on the earth have evolved various ways of coping with the wide range of temperatures found on our planet. During the earliest stages of the evolution of life, the conditions on earth were fairly uniform – warm and wet – and ideally suited to the small, primitive life forms then existing. As the climate changed and the different climatic zones already described began to form, the different species in them found several ways of adapting their bodies to their surrounding temperature.

Reptiles and insects warm up and cool down according to their environments. They become cold and torpid in cold temperatures and active, taking their heat from the sun, in warm ones. Mammals and birds, however, chose nature's version of an internal thermostat, that is, a fairly constant body temperature which varies slightly according to the species. The horse's average body temperature is about 38 °C or 100 °F, the dog's 38·3 °C or 101 °F and the human's 36·9 °C or 98·4 °F. Individuals will vary within the species and at different times of day and according to whether they are at rest or have been exercising, and temperature is slightly higher in the young than in the old.

It is crucial to the health and well-being of the body that the temperature remains very close to the individual's normal average. The body systems work best at that optimum temperature and variations can cause tissue damage and eventually death if prolonged. In fever conditions, a rise of only one degree may be enough to signify that something is going wrong; if the horse 'runs a temperature' of 40·5 °C (105 °F) for more than a few hours, life and future well-being are endangered, whether the cause is fever, or hyperthermia (over-heating) due to the weather or exercising.

Obviously, the ambient (surrounding) temperature is usually considerably lower than the normal body temperature, especially in winter, of course, so the horse's main problem is keeping his body temperature up to his optimum. He has various ways of doing this but none of them work without an adequate supply of energy in the form of food. Given a good diet to provide energy for the body's systems to work, the most obvious adaptation to the weather is the skin and, particularly, the coat. The blood circulation also changes to adapt to the temperature and the horse's instinct provides behavioural factors to complement the physical ones.

The 'thermostat' is the hypothalamus in the brain, which senses the temperature of the blood passing through it. Whether too hot or too cold, the hypothalamus sends out messages via the nervous system to set in motion the various systems and switch them off again when they are no longer needed.

At all times of year, the healthy functioning of the horse's skin and coat is vital to his life. It protects the underlying structures, is tough and elastic, having enormous tensile strength, can repair itself, enables the horse to make vitamin D from sunlight because of the reaction of ultra-violet light with substances in the skin, helps to keep the horse's body temperature constant despite outside conditions, helps him to excrete waste products via sweat, protects him from over-exposure to toxic substances, germs, water and foreign bodies and, because of its sensory capabilities, enables him to tell the difference between friction and pressure, heat and cold, pleasure and pain and provides some defence from insects.

It can, obviously, be injured, but a healthy skin can withstand assault from physical agents like wire, sticks and stones or whatever not only because of its elastic properties but because of its healing properties.

Skin consists of two main layers, the under layer or dermis and the top layer or epidermis, which itself has a thin top layer of insensitive, dead cells constantly shed as dandruff.

The dermis contains the hair follicles, sweat and oil glands, capillaries (tiny blood vessels) and nerve endings. It also contains the colouring agent melanin which, apart from giving the skin its colour, seems to have a strengthening effect on the skin and helps to protect it from sunlight, water and chemicals. It is said that washing white socks (which have pink skin under them without melanin) is the reason white-legged horses are more prone to mud fever, but this is only an exacerbating factor. Horses whose white socks are never washed get mud fever much more easily on their white socks than on their normally coloured legs. Also, horses grazing nitrogen-rich pasture in sunny weather get a sunburn-like condition on their white noses but not on, for example, their coloured chins.

The skin layers are joined together by little lumps or papillae which protrude from the dermis and fit into corresponding hollows on the underside of the epidermis. The dermis in turn is attached to white, tough tissue called connective tissue in various parts of the body, in fact more or less all over, and this obviously keeps it in place and stops it stretching and sagging down round the fetlocks! Because of the skin's elasticity, the horse can move quite comfortably in his 'elastic envelope'.

Skin can be up to about 6 mm thick in cold-blooded (northern-type) breeds of horse and pony over the top of the neck, back, loins and quarters, which are areas taking the brunt of the weather and needing to be less sensitive than parts such as the muzzle and legs, where skin is thinner. Southern-type animals, originating in hotter climes, have generally thinner skin.

Thinner skin also loses heat more quickly. Although desert animals do experience very cold nights, most of the time they are subject to extremely hot conditions and their thin skin helps them to tolerate this. Thicker-skinned animals often find hot conditions difficult to bear but conserve heat more effectively in cold weather than their thin-skinned relatives.

The body cools itself, or conserves heat, by means of the blood. When it is overheated, the blood capillaries in the skin and the vessels just under it dilate or widen to allow more heat-carrying blood near the surface of the body. The heat radiates out through the skin and is lost to the atmosphere. But in cold weather those vessels contract or narrow themselves, reducing the amount of blood in them and therefore the amount of heat that can escape. The vessels may even shut down completely, albeit temporarily, if the horse feels cold enough.

The horse's build also determines his ability to conserve or lose heat. It is usually found that hot-blooded, southern-type animals and their crosses have rather slimmer, more oval-shaped abdomens than colder-blooded, native-type animals, who tend to be rounder in the barrel. Heat is lost much more slowly from a barrel than from, say, a radiator, where the heat-containing fluid (whether it be blood, water or whatever) is near the surface of that radiator. A theory which is often quoted is that the amount of surface area (of skin) presented by the horse to the outside in relation to his height governs heat loss and conservation. It is said that the greater the skin surface the easier it is to lose heat. In practice, however – at least in my experience – this theory does not stand up too well. There are also too many other variables to be able to do accurate tests. A much better guide is the actual *type* (northern or southern) of the horse or pony's predominant characteristics.

The hair coat which covers the skin plays a most important part in heat retention and release. The roots of the hairs have attached to them tiny erector muscles which, on receiving a signal from the brain, can contract and pull the hair upwards, 'fluffing' out the coat as a bird does its feathers. As the winter coat is, of course, longer than the summer one anyway, and therefore thicker because the longer the hairs the more they overlap each other, it traps more air between the hairs next to the skin. Air is a great insulator and this is a significant aid in conserving heat – on a still day or in sheltered places.

When the wind blows, it parts the hair and allows the warm air to escape, so the horse feels colder. When the coat is wet from rain or sweat, things are even worse. The moisture flattens the hair, making the formation of the air layer impossible, so the horse does feel quite cold even on a still day. Water is a good conductor of heat, so heat is conducted away from the body via the wet skin. Heat is also lost by evaporation of the moisture if the surrounding air is dry enough. If the horse is sweating after work or if he is wet from rain, the effect is the same – flat, wet coat, rapid evaporation of moisture and corresponding heat loss causes one cold horse. The horse sweats because the expenditure of energy creates heat. This is one of the body's mechanisms to get rid of excess heat. It is not the act of sweating which cools the horse down but the evaporation and carrying away with the moisture of heat. This is necessary in an overheated horse to maintain the body temperature within its optimum range near the average.

If the horse is wet, however, and particularly if the wind is blowing, or if there is even a slight breeze or draught in a draughty box, the horse will have reached his normal temperature before he is dry if he has a long winter coat. But heat loss continues because of the wet, the air movement and the resulting natural radiation, conduction and convection of heat away from the horse's body. Then he is highly likely to get a sudden chill. Apart from stressing the body generally, chills can reduce the horse's natural resistance to infection and, if allowed to continue, can bring on hypothermia. We hear a lot about hypothermia these days, particularly in relation to old people, but anyone, including horses, can get hypothermia if the conditions are right.

If our wet horse is not sheltered and attended to, his body temperature will continue to drop until he becomes hypothermic. His temperature is lower than the optimum range and his body functions are difficult, or impossible, to maintain. Death, as we all know, can result.

If we clip the horse so that we reduce sweating and enable him to work with less risk of sweating too much, we remove the natural insulating hair layer. The wet horse can be dried off quicker and chilling risks reduced, but if, for example, the horse has been galloping or otherwise working hard on a cold winter's day *and is then allowed to stand around in the cold*, particularly if there is a breeze or wind blowing, his short, almost non-existent, coat will permit heat to be lost even faster than his long, wet coat would have done, and he will chill even faster and be in a more sudden danger of hypothermia.

The answer is to throw a rug over him and keep him moving around – one or the other and preferably both to be safe. This walking around also keeps the circulation moving faster than if he were standing still and allows the toxic waste products produced as his body 'burned' up fuel during work to be cleared out of his system (mostly by the kidneys). If the horse just stood still, the toxins could accumulate in the muscles, or at least not be removed quickly enough, and muscle damage, among other problems, could result.

One of the reasons northern-type animals sweat less readily than southern ones is because they are less sensitive to the hormones which trigger off the sweating process. They do not need to be because, in their natural environment, they do not need to sweat so much. Then, when we have an absolute heatwave they can really suffer. My local veterinary surgeon reported more cases of hyperthermia (the opposite of hypothermia) during the heatwave of 1976 (and a subsequent one a few years later) than he had ever known, all in British native-bred ponies and cold-blooded horses such as Cleveland Bays and Shires.

This effect of air movement (wind) on a wet horse, or even a dry one, is called the wind-chill factor. We in Britain first became generally familiar with this expression from media weather forecasts during the Great Freeze of January 1987. Even the sound of it made us shiver! But what does it mean exactly – in simple terms? Well, much of its principle has been explained in the preceding paragraphs, without using the actual expression. The wind hastens the rate at which heat is convected or blown by air movement away from the body so you (or your horse) feel chillier faster, and the body has to burn up fuel faster to keep its temperature at the right level. If the speed of heat loss is faster than the body can produce heat, if the exposure to wind chill is prolonged and the body's fuel stocks are insufficient, the body temperature cannot be kept up and the horse could die.

Possessing a generous layer of fat does help to insulate the horse to some extent and does provide fuel supplies to call on in emergency or periods of extra demand such as during particularly severe weather or an inadequate diet. Horses should go into the winter well covered without being gross if they are to be significantly exposed to winter weather. Working horses such as hunters, racehorses and point-to-pointers must obviously not carry much spare fat but are also not turned out for many hours at a time. They often wear clothing at exercise and are clipped and rugged up in the stable. What can happen with these horses, however, is that they are roughed off too quickly in early spring, when the weather can still be bitter, and are not allowed to fatten up a bit before going out, then they lose flesh (muscle) as opposed to fat (of which there is none spare) trying to combat the effects of the cold to which they have suddenly been exposed by incompetent or uncaring human connections. The body is using up its own tissues as fuel.

Naturally, such horses can become hypothermic, extremely thin even if given supplementary feeding, and can die. It may sound fantastic to think that valuable horses like this can be treated so, but it does happen.

Wind chill, then, only works on a source of heat such as a living body. The wind cannot chill a warm object to a lower temperature than the surrounding air; it simply brings it to that temperature quicker than on a still day. If heat continues to be produced, as discussed above, the process will take longer. In a living creature the body will work to combat the chill as best it can, as described.

A 30-mph wind (not all that strong) in an air temperature of $-5\,°C$ ($23\,°F$) produces the same chilling effect on the body as an air temperature of $-25\,°C$ ($-13\,°F$) on a still day. In the battle against winter weather, our main enemies are wind and wet, not cold alone.

Shivering is one of the horse's keep-warm mechanisms. It causes the muscles to move and movement creates warmth, but this is one instance where nature does not do too well. A shivering horse should not be left to get on with it in the belief that the shivering will warm him up any more than it does us. If he is shivering, he should be warmed up by rubbing and massage, clothing and a warm feed, even though the effect of the latter will be temporary. It will at least act as an emergency comfort and heat source for him.

In cases where the horse comes out into cold sweats for whatever reason, maybe shock after an accident, or exhaustion, he should be clothed with an anti-sweat rug and warm clothing on top as he will obviously lose further body heat because of the moisture. Veterinary advice should be sought in these cases.

Finally, the effects of a good, full tail should not be underestimated in heat conservation. The mane helps a little to keep heat from being lost excessively from the radiator-like neck, but it is the quarters which the horse turns to the wind to protect the more vulnerable front end from heat loss. The muscular quarters act as a windbreak for the forehand, but the skin between the buttocks and hind legs, and on the belly, is thin and heat is easily lost from it.

The purpose of the tail is to shield these areas, but if we pull the tail and clip up round the sides of the dock we leave those areas almost completely exposed. Research work done in America showed that, given two groups of horses of the same type, kept under the same conditions, those with the unpulled tails retained body condition much better than those with pulled tails. The latter were using up body fuel to keep up with the heat lost from those thin-skinned areas exposed by trimming the tails. Apart from the practical considerations, it is cruel intentionally to expose horses to winter conditions without at least allowing them the protection nature gave them or providing an adequate substitute in the form of a tail flap on a turn-out rug of some kind.

3 Shelter and Housing

I hope the explanations of body temperature and the effects on it of wind and wet will have made clear the need for proper shelter from the elements if a horse is not only to feel more comfortable but do well, too.

Horses do survive in very varied conditions in the world but in nearly all of them there are *some* natural shelter facilities to enable them to protect themselves from harsh weather. The sad sight so often seen in domesticity of horses – or, even sadder, a lone horse – standing with their tails to a post-and-rail or wire fence or, at best, a straggly, thin bush or hedge proves the fact that horses *will* seek shelter when conditions are bad and that it is quite unnatural, and stressful, for them to suffer exposure with no means of avoiding the wind and wet which cause them so much discomfort.

Natural – truly natural – shelter consists of forests and woods, cliffs and canyons and valleys, natural shrubbery, gulleys and dips in the ground, all of which the animals can use to get something between them and the weather, if not completely, at least to the extent that the worst effects are warded off. They have access not only to windbreak-type shelter from the side but to overhead shelter to protect them from excessive rain and snow.

Obviously, the type of conditions in which many domesticated animals are kept – a comparatively small field with man-made fencing or at best natural but too-low hedges – are quite inadequate when compared to natural shelter. The horse's coat can only offer *partial* protection from the weather, and this is not enough.

Horses living in wild, natural conditions have certain behavioural, and doubtless some learned, methods of avoiding the brunt of the elements. Their stance is one: as described previously, they stand with their quarters and tails to the weather to protect the more sensitive forehand. They do not stand broadside to it because this would present a large body area to the cold, so correspondingly more heat would be lost from the body. By standing with the 'narrow end' to the weather, that much less skin surface is exposed to it, so more heat is conserved. Cold or sheltering horses also usually bunch together to get the benefit of each other's body heat and the coating of mud they give themselves when they roll, although at first seeming to be counter-productive because it appears to destroy the insulating air layer in the coat, does, in fact, harden on to provide solid protection which is highly effective against wind. It seems that horses coat their sides with mud instinctively to give that broad skin area more protection.

Many horse owners have little choice over the grazing conditions of their horses and ponies because they do not have their own facilities. If any choice at all is available, it is worth spending some time yourself in the paddocks intended for winter turn-out facilities, either long or short term, and trying to get some idea of the lie of the land before choosing a field. Is the paddock directly in the path of the prevailing wind of the district or north and east winds, or is it sheltered by nearby higher ground, a spinney or even a housing estate? Is there a gulley down the middle of it down which the wind will be channelled, or is it cross-ways to the main wind direction, so offering some shelter from it? Is whatever natural shelter and hedging there is between the paddock (and therefore the horses) and the wind, or will the wind (and whatever it is blowing with it in the way of rain, sleet, hail and snow) meet the horses first because there is nothing on that side to stop it? Can the horses get to overhead shelter in that spinney or is it fenced off? If there is a gate, do they really know where it is – and is the spinney safe or are there traps set in it? Is the paddock on the top of a windswept rise or hill or in a sheltered but waterlogged valley bottom?

It sounds complicated, and, indeed, it does take a little hard thinking and maybe a new way of looking at your countryside, before you can really decide what real natural shelter there is. But it will pay dividends in the shape of your horses' comfort, well-being and body condition – and ultimately in your feed and veterinary bills because the worse your horse feels, the more run-down in health he will become, requiring more food to keep condition on him, and the lower will be his resistance to disease because his resources will all be going on fighting the weather.

Domestic shelter conditions such as planted or remaining natural woodlands, and also hedgerows if allowed to grow high and thick right to the ground, are excellent and will be gratefully used by the horses. Woods must, however, be regularly checked for traps and snares set by poachers. If game have been reared in them, equipment used for that must be removed, otherwise inquisitive horses might interfere with it and damage both it and themselves. I know of two ponies recently who were poisoned by nibbling the roofing felt on pheasant housing and one which cut its leg very badly on a hopper feeder left in a spinney.

Failing adequate natural shelter, the obvious solution is a man-made field shelter. An open-fronted, three-sided shed with a single-plane roof sloping to the back can be made by any reasonably competent handyman from used timber. The four corner posts should be sunk into the ground for one-third of their length (following treatment with preservative), maybe in concrete-filled holes for extra strength, but no other foundation or flooring is necessary. The open front means there is no *cul-de-sac* for one horse to be cornered by another and bullied. The shed should be sited with its back to the prevailing wind or, if there is no obvious wind direction in the area, with its back to the north or east. If the wind does change direction, the horses will simply shelter behind the shed until it changes back again.

The best shelters form three-quarters of a circle with the opening on the remaining quarter. These allow a pestered horse to run round the inside and out of the opening, when necessary, but offer shelter on all four sides.

The site for the shelter should be carefully chosen: it must be on the highest and driest area of the field to prevent the inside becoming waterlogged from rainwater running into it. Do not site it too near a fence or other solid object; it is best to leave a clear passage of several yards round it so that horses milling around have space to manoeuvre and will not become trapped and injured.

Wood is the material of choice for field shelters. Materials which are good conductors of heat such as metal or asbestos should be avoided if at all possible, especially for the roof, as they will be freezing in winter and stifling in summer even with the open front. Provided they are securely fixed with timber cross-posts, adequate shelters can be made simply by stacking straw bales like brickwork and battening on a slightly sloping roof covered with roofing felt (provided this is well out of reach of the horses).

As for dimensions, roughly 18 ft (about 5·5 m) by 12 ft (3·6 m) by 10 ft (3 m) high is adequate for two horses. Good friends may well manage with a smaller shelter. For each additional animal, add about 6 ft (2 m) to the length.

An interesting observation was made in *Equine Behaviour*, the journal of the Equine Behaviour Study Circle, by a member who had been studying her horses' behaviour. She has loose boxes in her field kept open for her horses to come and go as they wish, and a normal shelter. She found that friendly horses were often happy to share one normal-size box while the boss horse had the neighbouring one to himself next door. If, however, the three of them had to use the same, *un*partitioned shelter, despite the extra space available, the boss horse chivvied the other two and gave them no peace. It seems that when they used separate boxes (two in one, one in the other), although they could get at each other through the open doors, no bullying occurred and they were happy in their 'private rooms'.

This is a point well worth considering where several horses are turned out together or where there is any situation in which one horse might be kept out of the shelter by others. Two shelters, or a larger divided one would be the answer if adequate facilities are to be provided for all concerned.

Sometimes it is possible to use an old barn or other farm building which does duty as a covered yard and which opens directly into a field, and this, because of the extra size usually involved, can make a really excellent facility.

A *very* common remark in the horse world is: 'My horse won't use a shelter.' Just about *every* horse will use a shelter (a) when he feels the need and (b) provided he is not afraid to do so. Horses can be frightened of using or even approaching a shelter by all sorts of things, the most common being other, superior status horses keeping them out, badly poached or rough ground on the approach to the shelter, a dark and/or low, narrow entrance so the horse either cannot see where he is going or what is inside or is afraid of knocking his head, withers or hips negotiating the entrance, rattling building materials as caused by a loose panel or a tree branch constantly blowing against the roof or wall, memories of past injuries caused in or near shelters, flapping polythene nearby and lack of space inside.

The remedy to most of these causes is obvious. As for bad memories, if you ensure that his companion/s are either inferior to him in the herd pecking order or that they are best friends and if you lead him into the shelter yourself, fussing him, being confident and offering him a scrumptious feed inside, he probably will overcome his fear in time, especially if you make a point of checking him over in the shelter and handling him in there daily. Keep the shelter bedded down on deep litter (droppings being meticulously removed at least once a day and fresh bedding added as necessary) to make it welcoming, and scatter some bedding in the entrance as a 'welcome mat'. Also, fix wall-type hayracks along the back wall (the long cattle type being excellent for this) at horse's head height or only just above to avoid injury, and keep them fully stocked with good hay, hay-age or whatever roughage you normally feed, and the shelter will become a real haven to your horses where they know they will find food and comfort, to the benefit of their condition and your peace of mind.

Simple roofless windbreaks can be erected in paddocks which will help to break the force of the wind and/or give horses something to shelter behind. If the shape is carefully thought out, they can be constructed so as to offer shelter from all directions. They can be made of second-hand timber or, in fact, any material at all which is rigid enough to avoid flapping around and which can be fixed to support-posts sunk into the ground. Again, they should be on the driest part of the field.

In an exposed paddock, a high fence comprising wooden posts and very close mesh, heavy-duty plastic can be erected on the windward border of the land. This breaks the force of the wind in much the same way as a hedge or shelter belt and is an excellent measure to implement, especially while waiting for natural shelter such as hedges and trees to grow. The fence also offers some protection to young plants and so encourages quicker growth.

If you have your own land or have the use of it for a period of years such as on a long lease, it is well worth planting hedges and trees to form shelter belts.

Probably the best species for hedges are hawthorn and blackthorn. Unfortunately they take a very long time to grow and some faster-growing species should also be incorporated if you want to see fairly prompt results to your labours or commissioned work. As for trees, which can be incorporated into hedges either to be allowed to grow as trees or to form the hedges themselves, the fastest-growing native species is alder which, however, grows best on damp land. Sycamore is regarded by many conservationists as a weed, but grow fast it certainly does! No matter what the conservationists say, it still provides habitat, shade and shelter to wildlife and horses alike and in exposed areas of land whose owners are in a hurry (relatively) to produce natural shelter, I think there is a very good case for planting sycamore.

Poisonous growths of various kinds are often attracted by

hedges, and the list of poisonous plants in Britain is quite alarming. Common hedgerow poisonous plants include nightshades, foxgloves, bryony, mare's tail and wild arum. Poisonous tree species include yew (absolutely deadly), oak (because of the acorns), horse chestnut (because of the conkers), privet, rhododendron, laurel, laburnum (although this is unlikely to be used as a hedge, its proximity to a horse paddock should be avoided) and box.

May and beech can be used to form part of your hedge and copper beech, in particular, looks lovely as well as providing practical service.

If the above mention of poisonous things makes you feel it is not worth the risk, if you plant the correct tree/hedge species in the first place and systematically get rid of poisonous plants as part of your grassland management, you should not have a problem. Most poisonous things taste horrible, in any case (so they tell me!), and horses only usually nibble them when really hungry. If you keep your horses well fed and never allow them to get into that highly unnatural state (for horses) again, you will be at low risk from poisoning.

Once maturing well, hedges benefit greatly from being professionally trimmed and laid, which involves partially hacking through the trunks of the trees and laying them in a diagonal direction, securing the tops with a braid of branches. This process needs doing perhaps once in a generation on a large scale. Periodic attention to the work due to natural growth will be needed every ten years or so, and the hedge should be trimmed in early September every year or two. Such a hedge provides a valuable windbreak and stock-proof fence as well as being a highway and habitat for wildlife.

Advice on species to plant and contractors to do the work can be obtained from the Agricultural Development Advisory Service (ADAS) department of your local Ministry of Agriculture, Fisheries and Food (address in the phone book).

It will be necessary to protect your young trees and hedges from the horses while they are growing. A fence (temporary, maybe) should be erected about a metre inside the hedge to stop the horses eating the young trees, and the trunks of mature trees should have a guard round them (if only securely fixed chicken wire) to stop the horses stripping the bark off and killing the trees.

Stabling is, of course, the ultimate 'shelter'. Many horses who are out a good deal for most of the year often find themselves stabled during winter more than at any other time. There is no doubt that horses come to regard their stables as the place to be when everything is right with the world. Most of them feel that it is 'home base'; they feel safe in there, they associate the stable with food, comfort, safety and security, but that does not mean they do not want to go out, of course, either for work or in the paddock for some much-needed freedom.

Unfortunately, some stables are so bad for their occupants' health that they should carry a Government health warning. The main problem is lack of ventilation and all types of stabling can suffer from this, from stalls to loose boxes, indoor and out. If the air-space and air-change is insufficient to maintain fresh, pure air, the stabling, no matter how many 'mod cons' it may possess, is not only inadequate but bad for your horse's health. And size alone is not a guarantee that air quality will be good enough.

Obviously, the longer a horse is stabled, the more water vapour, carbon dioxide (from the lungs), ammonia (from the urine) and methane (from decomposing organic matter and wind expelled from the anus) are excreted into the stable, among other more minor contaminants. In addition, there may well be dust, which is a physical irritant to the lungs, either from the general surroundings or from hay and straw, and, also from the latter two, fungal spores. This is quite an army of contamination working against your horse's health and comfort, and which he would never come up against outside (unless his hay and straw were significantly dusty or mouldy). The heat from his own body, his perspiration (which goes on unnoticed in a resting horse) and the water vapour from his lungs combine to make an unhealthy humid atmosphere. Methane is toxic and ammonia is caustic. All mucous membranes can be affected, those usually succumbing first being the lungs and eyes. Horses with sensitive skin come up with apparently inexplicable skin disorders, coughing is common even in horses not susceptible to COPD and in the latter their breathing becomes so difficult that they cannot work and in extreme cases become likely candidates for heart failure. Exercise-induced pulmonary haemorrhage (EIPH) or nose bleeds result from inflamed lungs and the warmth, moisture and availability of organic material provide a haven for breeding bacteria and viruses of many kinds. Poor ventilation can even bring on foal pneumonia.

The ammonia (being a heavy gas) and water vapour stay at a low level near or on the floor and bedding – exactly where resting, sleeping horses and foals are breathing – while the warm air rises, creating lack of oxygen in badly ventilated, too-low stables. This sort of atmosphere gives humans a dozy, headachy feeling and who is to say that it does not affect horses that way, too? In addition, the warm, damp air helps to rot the building itself.

This sort of thing happens in *all* stabling where ventilation is poor. 'Outdoor' loose boxes where the horse can put his head directly outside offer the horse some relief, but only as long as his head is out. The fact that his top door is open, and maybe the window (which is invariably on the same side), does not ensure adequate ventilation, particularly in most makes of prefabricated loose box which almost always have too-low roofs.

In indoor loose boxes constructed inside another building, as in the American barn system or any indoor conversion, the problem can be much worse as stagnant, sometimes putrid, air pools inside the boxes while clean air may be blowing down the aisle unable to get into the actual boxes.

The latter type of stabling may need complex and costly ventilation systems comprising vents and electrically operated extraction fans, installed under the supervision of a ventilation expert. Indoor boxes sited round indoor schools, sharing their open space, are particularly bad as the dust unavoidably generated by working horses in all but the most frequently and thoroughly watered schools is constantly present in detectable quantities in the air.

I always think it strange that establishments which insist on their staff wearing face masks during such jobs as filling haynets and mucking out stables think nothing of giving their horses that very same hay to eat and making them spend up to twenty-two hours out of twenty-four in those very same stables!

You can easily test your stable's ventilation quality yourself. Spend some time outdoors, then go into your horse's stable and breathe in slowly and deeply, noting whether the air smells or feels noticeably different from that outside. If it does, you have ventilation problems. Sit down on the floor and read a book or something and stay there for at least half an hour. Can you breathe quite comfortably or do you notice a quite unpleasant smell of dust, ammonia or warm horse with an 'off' tang to it? Is the damp seeping through your clothing? Are your eyes beginning to water? Do you feel you would like some fresh air? Or do you want to clear your throat, blow your nose or, heaven forbid, cough? If you can answer an honest 'no' to all those questions, you, and your horse, are in the clear – literally. Otherwise, you know that you have to do something about it. Other signs of something amiss are condensation on windows or metal structures or on your spectacles if you wear them. Even if your horse is not already broken-winded (suffering from COPD) such conditions could well favour its development. Horses in such an environment are continually under stress fighting off the effects of a bad atmosphere and using up their body resources to do so, when they should be going to fight off *unusual* attacks from outside influences or put into work.

Leaving the top door open *is*, indeed, one way to help bring in more fresh air and let out stale air. The problem is ensuring good ventilation, especially in winter, without causing draughts. A too-rapid airflow will certainly do that. Size plays an important part in air-change requirements. For a horse of about 16 hands high, a box about 12 ft square (about 4 m square) by the same distance to the eaves is large enough to allow frequent air change without draughts. In stables with ceilings or single-plane roofs, the height should be a good 2 ft (0·6 m) higher.

Ventilation devices such as ridge roof cupolas should ideally extend the full length of the roof, not just for a short distance, there should be gable-end louvres (which should be kept clear and open) and there should be windows or louvres on *both* sides of the stable, not just on the same side as the door, to create a clearing cross-flow of air. This, of course, is just as welcome in summer, when excess heat is a problem, as in winter, when horses stabled for many hours need regular air-change in their boxes.

Ventilation experts tell us that a floor-level grilled inlet for air is necessary on the side opposite the door to create a floor-level flow of air to help clear away that ammonia, but I have never yet managed to get a satisfactory answer out of one of them to explain how we then avoid floor draughts!

Of course, if the ammonia is not allowed to build up in the first place because the stable is scrupulously cleaned out every day, there will be no problem, but working owners who keep their horses on deep litter or semi-deep litter may genuinely not have time for this. (There is more on this topic in Chapter 8.)

Good drainage will prevent excess urine from building up and giving off smells, but bedding will soak up most urine anyway, even straw which is said to be a 'drainage' (in other words, non-absorbent) bedding, especially today's straw which is mangled and crushed up during baling. Good ventilation, then, is especially important where deep litter systems are used.

Electricity supplies to stable yards and buildings are a 'mod con' most owners would not dream of being without; they have become a present-day basic necessity and life would certainly be harder without them. They can, however, cause problems, but if correctly installed and maintained they are quite safe. Obviously, basic safety insists that horses should not be able to interfere with electrical fittings in any way. Cables should run inside metal conduits, preferably the type which fit flush across a corner to avoid a sharp edge being created, or a projection which a possibly bored, inquisitive horse can investigate with its teeth.

Lights should be the non-corrosive, waterproof bulkhead type and be fixed well up out of reach of the horses, and switches should be waterproof and fitted, where loose boxes are concerned, outside the box away from the reach of the horse or, in barn-type stabling, at each end of the aisles.

Lighting is a subject which receives little attention, but I feel it worth mentioning that fluorescent lighting is known to cause severe headaches and dizziness in humans because it flickers on and off very rapidly – too rapidly for the eye really to detect, but the light waves it emits apparently conflict with the brain's own electrical waves. This is quite likely to happen with the normal, cheaper type of fluorescent light which only emits light from the blue end of the white-light spectrum. Full-spectrum fluorescent light, such as that used in greenhouses and aquaria, emits just that, full-spectrum red-to-blue light which is more natural and beneficial. In winter, when lights are on so much more, particularly in barn-type stabling, or when they are used to help bring mares into season, surely it would be much more effective and less harmful to install full-spectrum fluorescent tubes instead of the normal, coldly clinical blue-spectrum ones. Full-spectrum lighting has a beneficial effect on humans, too, creating the happier atmosphere of a spring day and none of the irritability brought on in 'sick building syndrome' which we hear so much about these days – due largely to blue-spectrum fluorescent lighting, among other things.

If you have no electricity supply in your stables, you will be denied such beneficial items as electric groomers, hot water and electrical clipping machines. You can, however, get a few storm lanterns to take into and out of stables with you, provided you have a safe recessed hook up high from which to hang them. At least you will not be worrying about electrical fires!

An excellent method of housing horses in extreme weather conditions, and one which is not used as much in Britain as it could be, is yarding them. Yards can be covered, open or, ideally, a combination of the two. They can be any convenient size, from a small barn to a large manège, and have a dirt floor or special flooring such as wood chips. The horses can come and go from shelter to yard as they please, have the benefit of natural social contact with other horses and space and freedom to move around. Because the floors are usually specially laid, there are no mud or waterlogging problems and horses are usually very happy with this arrangement. They can be fed communally or brought out if individual feeds need to be given and the method saves a great deal of time in mucking out stables. Droppings are removed from the yard and shelter area and the bedding in the latter kept on deep litter. Because the horses have access to the open air, or are in large covered areas, respiratory problems are not usually evident, but in wholly covered yards, ventilation must still be adequate or the same sort of problems will occur as in badly ventilated stabling.

Winter is a time when the horses of working owners may not be under as frequent supervision as in the summer unless at full livery. It is very tempting to visit an outdoor horse, for example, only once a day to give it a quick once-over and stock up the shelter with hay, but this really is not enough. Twice a day should be a minimum at any time of year, and, of course, if the horse is stabled, the time of year will not make any difference.

From a security point of view, many animals are stolen during the evening or very early morning prior to a sale in the region. Should a working owner, for example, omit to visit the horse in the morning before going to work, it could have been stolen, put through an auction and slaughtered before he or she even became aware at the following evening visit that it was missing. A morning visit would at least have alerted the owner to the fact that the horse was gone and steps could have been taken which might have recovered it before it was too late.

Unpleasant though freezing, black winter's mornings may be, and evenings, too, the safety and security of the horses remain just as vital as in summer, so winter visits and supervision should not be skimped. From the point of view of the horse's health, leaving a sick or injured horse for many hours, as would happen on a one-visit-a-day regime, could make the difference between spotting the condition in the first place and acting in time to ensure a quick recovery or, perhaps, losing the horse in, say, a case of serious colic.

Fencing and gates in winter often come in for more stress than in summer. In good grazing times, the horses are normally too busy eating to get up to mischief, but in winter, particularly if the hay stocks have run out, they start looking for something to do and begin chewing or testing the fences or milling around together and buffeting the fencing in the process. Also, gaps in hedges often become glaringly obvious because of the lack of foliage, and horses, and ponies in particular, often escape just for something interesting to do.

Fencing posts are the most important part of any fence. Without secure posts nothing you fasten to them will stay put and keep your horses in. Before winter sets in, check the fencing carefully and have any shaky posts put right, then carry out any necessary repairs to the rails, wire or hedge gaps and check the condition of gates. It does help to have gates properly hung so that, if you are feeding outdoor horses, you do not have to put everything down and keep picking it up again to open gates because it is a two-handed job to lift a stubborn gate out of the mud, heave it to one side, bring everything into the paddock, and put it all down again within reach of the horses (who will be only too keen to find out what is there) while you struggle with the gate again.

If the horses have become hungry, the gateway is often the place where they will congregate waiting for you, and the gate can come in for a good deal of pressure. Sliprails are cheaper than gates but not as secure when a small herd of fractious horses is putting them to the test. They must be really stout and securely fixed (probably screwed through the gateposts with strong nuts and smooth-headed bolts) to be of any use.

Although we do get our share of snow and frost in Britain, most of our winters are cold, windy and wet rather than below freezing for months, or even weeks, on end. Our main problem is mud rather than ice and snow.

A field intended for winter use must be well drained otherwise it will quickly turn into a morass of oozing, liquid mud not fit for anything, let alone accommodating horses. It should slope gently towards some outlet such as a ditch or stream or even a pond. If it is low lying and level it should have well-maintained ditches or dykes on all sides and these must be securely fenced off from the horses. Needless to say, a proper drainage system is an advantage to almost any field, but especially one meant for winter use.

Wet land does not support the best kinds of grasses for horses. In winter this does not matter because the grass is of no practical feeding value anyway, but you can tell from the types of grasses growing on a field at any time of year whether or not it is likely to become waterlogged in wet weather. If it supports clumps of round, spiky marsh grasses or, worse, rushes, you know the field is no good for your purposes.

The field must go into the winter with a good covering of grass. Do not choose one which has been grazed hard all summer as there will be no growth at all to offer a little protection to the soil from horses' hooves. The best types of grass to sow in a field for winter use are agrostis species as these are hardwearing and have good tillering (spreading) qualities. They do not have a high feeding value but, as mentioned, in winter this is unimportant.

Soil types are also significant. The worst type of soil is clay, which quickly turns into a stiff, holding goo which seems to cause mud fever quicker than anything else. The ideal is a light sandy soil which allows the water to drain more quickly through its coarser grains.

A winter field should be as large as possible to minimise poaching and subsequent possible skin problems and damage to future grass growth. The advice normally given about acreages for keeping horses at grass of two acres for the first horse and one for each subsequent horse are minimal for winter use if the animals are going to be out all the time. Aim for the largest, best drained, best covered and best sheltered field you can find for winter.

A big deciding factor will, of course, be whether or not the field has a suitable water source for the horses. Whereas in summer you may be able to bear rigging up a hosepipe to fill some portable container once or twice a day, in winter this task can become almost overwhelming, especially if you somehow forget to bring the hosepipe indoors one night and end up with it frozen next morning, resulting in no means of getting water to your horses. Laid on water with properly lagged pipes is really a necessity in winter.

Natural sources such as ponds can be dangerous. Pond water is frequently unfit to drink and ponds, streams and rivers can be polluted these days and have unsafe approaches. Even running water can freeze in winter. Horses can wander on to frozen ponds with fatal results. A proper trough is best with some automatic filling device. If the field is near the yard, a hosepipe and plastic dustbin rammed into a tractor tyre and tied to the fence would do well enough.

If the horses are not going to be out all the time, but just turned out for a few hours, you may not need a water source at all, provided the horses are amply watered at other times. Most stabled horses have water with them all the time nowadays.

Water supplies to stables are, of course, just as prone to freezing as supplies in fields. It really is worth having the pipes well lagged with almost anything you can find – old sacking, blankets or rugs will do if you have no proper lagging material – to avoid the considerable inconvenience of being frozen up.

Thermostats are available for automatic waterers and you can also buy pipe-heating kits (companies marketing heater kits advertise in most horse magazines during autumn and winter). Remember, you do not need or want the water to be actually warm, just to remain a few degrees above freezing. Horses' natural tendency is not to drink so much in winter. They also may come to no harm if the water is very cold, but they will certainly drink far more if it is a more comfortable temperature, to the benefit of their health.

Outside sources can have a plastic football floated on top of the water. The constant slight movement in the breeze and as horses drink prevents freezing in a not-too-severe freeze. Insulated containers are also available, but you can rig up your own by using a large plastic container with a slightly smaller one inside it (such as two dustbins) and filling the space between them with straw or hay, which does help to delay freezing.

Stable water containers can have a thin layer of rigid plastic floated on top to prevent freezing. The horses soon learn to push it down to drink.

4 Feeding and Watering

Any system, biological or mechanical, gives more efficient and longer service if it is used and maintained according to its design, and this is equally true of the horse's digestive system.

The horse is a herbivore or vegetarian, that is, it eats plant material for nourishment rather than other animal's bodies, as do carnivores. Although carnivores have the disadvantage of having to hunt their food, that food is so much more concentrated than plant material that one large feed every day (if they are fortunate), or even every few days, is quite enough to keep them well fed.

In the wild, horses' food is all around them (except in times of severe drought or in a normal winter when it has little nourishment in it and may be covered by several inches or even feet of snow, or frozen hard). Normally, they can eat at will, walking slowly around and cropping grass or browsing leaves from shrubs and trees, as they wish. Plant material is variable in content throughout the year but it is always much less concentrated than meat. In order to obtain sufficient nourishment from it, horses have to eat very large quantities and inevitably take in with the nourishment vast amounts of bulk fibrous roughage in the form of the cellulose and woody material called lignin which makes up the substance of vegetation. Some of this roughage can be digested and made use of but much cannot.

However, the horse's digestive system evolved over many millions of years to accept, cope with and ultimately need this roughage to bulk out the intestines, stimulate the intestinal movements (peristalsis) which push the food along the tract and physically break up the more concentrated parts of the horse's diet. Without adequate roughage in its diet, the horse not only feels uncomfortably empty and hungry, but its digestive system cannot work properly and indigestion can result. Indigestion can range from mild discomfort to serious disorder. Chronic indigestion can cause such so-called vices as wood-chewing and crib-biting, over-nervousness or temperament problems.

The horse, however, unlike the cow, is not a ruminant. It does not have a rumen for storage and partial processing of its food until it is convenient to 'chew its cud'. Horses have very specialised digestive systems with small stomachs in relation to their size, compared with carnivores which have large stomachs to take a very large, occasional meal. The horse's intestinal tract is capacious to cope with the natural bulky food it is 'designed' to live on, and it is also sensitive, requiring only good-quality food. It needs a small amount of food passing almost constantly through it: in natural conditions horses and their relatives (asses and zebras) eat for about sixteen hours a day and sometimes more if the food content of their available fodder is low.

Mammals use food for four main purposes. In order of importance, they are:

1. Maintenance of body temperature, which is vital to the efficient working of body functions, as explained previously.
2. Manufacture of new body tissue (organs, muscles, skin, horn, etc.) to allow for growth and development in the young and to replace that used daily in all animals.
3. Maintaining body condition or weight. Food excess to immediate needs is stored around the body as fat reserves. Those under the skin around the outside of the body help to protect the inner parts from cold, so if a horse is thin from illness or malnutrition or carrying no surplus fat because he is fit, he will feel the cold more than his chubbier colleagues.
4. Provision of energy for movement and life, from winning

the Derby to swishing his tail at a fly, and for the working of the body's systems (circulation, respiration, digestion itself, etc.).

Because requirement number 1 is paramount, it is obviously critical in winter to feed to keep out the cold, as it were, as well as for the other purposes. The horse's body allocates its food (or fuel) supplies in order of priority. If the food eaten only just accounts for requirements 1 and 2, for example, there will be little or none left for number 3 and the horse will be thin with no fat reserves to help ward off the cold. He will also have little to spare for requirement 4 and will be weak and listless.

Should the food not even account for requirements 1 and 2, the body, having no appreciable fat reserves to call on, will start using up its own flesh as fuel and the horse will eventually become emaciated, incapable of retaining its body temperature and die.

This process can happen at any time of year, but will do so quicker in winter – unless the horse dies of hypothermia first.

Obviously, the horse requires feeding all the time whether working or resting. Feeding an out-of-work horse enough to keep him 'ticking over' and in healthy condition is called feeding for maintenance, a maintenance ration normally being 2 per cent of the horse's bodyweight for ponies, 2½ per cent for horses and 3 per cent for youngstock and brood mares etc. The subject of feeding according to bodyweight was touched on in Chapter 1 in relation to feeding youngstock. A measuring tape was recommended which enables the owner or manager to calculate the horse's bodyweight and a resulting total amount of feed per day. If such a tape is not immediately available and a quick decision needs to be made, the following formula can be operated by using an ordinary tape measure or a piece of string and measuring that.

Take the horse or pony's measurement round the girth (just behind the withers) and its length from the point of the shoulder to the point of the buttock. Then apply this formula: girth multiplied by girth, multiplied by the length, the result divided by 300, and 50 added to that. This will give you the animal's weight in pounds. This works well with an animal in fair body condition, that is, not too thin and not too fat. It obviously takes no account of whether the animal is a good doer or not when working out the resulting weight of food per day. The eye of the master still comes into play and common sense should be used. However, it is a fairly accurate guide which can be modified by experience and in the light of knowledge of the individual horse.

If, for example, your horse weighs 1000 lbs, feeding him for maintenance would mean giving him a total of 20 lbs of food daily. This could be fed as all roughage (hay or equivalent) if the quality is good, or, depending on the individual, up to one-third could be fed as concentrates (straight grain, cubes, coarse mix, etc.). This might be particularly appropriate in cold weather.

Feeding for work involves providing enough food for the extra energy required (requirement number 4) without the horse losing weight. Light work can be performed on a 2 per cent of bodyweight ration (say 45 minutes daily walking with an occasional trot), medium to hard work on a 2·5 per cent of bodyweight ration and strenuous work such as racing, three-day eventing or endurance riding on a 2·5–3 per cent of bodyweight ration.

The roughage:concentrate ratio also has an effect. Obviously, if the horse is receiving all his ration as roughage, as he might on a maintenance ration, unless that roughage is top class he will not be capable of much physical effort in the way of work – although it *is* perfectly possible to work horses hard on really top-class hay and little else. If the ratio (but not the percentage of bodyweight) were changed, so that the horse received his ration as two-thirds roughage and one-third concentrates, he would be capable of more work.

In harder work, the percentage would be raised so that the horse could be on a 2·5 per cent of bodyweight ration but still on a split of two-thirds roughage, one-third concentrates. As the work becomes more demanding, it is usual to change the ratio first before increasing the bodyweight percentage. Therefore the horse in heavy work might be receiving half his ration as roughage and the other half as concentrates. Ultimately, horses in strenuous work could have their roughage reduced to not less than a third of their total ration with concentrates at two-thirds. In the latter case, the horse, depending on his individual requirement for food in general, might be on a 3 per cent of bodyweight ration (which would also be applicable to youngstock and lactating mares).

Hard-working horses in winter are rarely kept out, or turned out for long periods exposed to the cold, but it should be remembered when deciding on a diet that exposure to cold increases food requirements, in addition to those required for work, so the foregoing percentages and ratios should be increased and changed accordingly. No precise details can be given because of individual horses' turn-out and work arrangements, clothing worn and their individual tolerance of weather, but I hope the information given will prove a reliable guide.

Although dividing a ration fairly scientifically up into roughage:concentrate ratios and applying different formulae is an accurate method of gauging needs, a method of feeding which works particularly well for animals of all types, except possibly the very greedy, is to feed as much good hay (or hay equivalent) as they want and to 'build up' concentrates on top of that ration as needed. When feeding this way, I have found almost invariably that animals often come up themselves with the rations and ratios just detailed unless exceptionally good hay is being fed; then I have found that horses can work hard enough for demanding sports such as long-distance riding and point-to-pointing with very few concentrates. If the hay is of good, but not super, quality, the roughage:concentrate ratio of about 70:30 seems to be 'decided' by the horses themselves when out a good deal in winter or working moderately to hard – an interesting verification of the more scientific method.

Giving animals a fairly constant supply of fodder (hay) in winter, particularly when out and during the night (whether stabled or not) is a good way to create body heat and keep them warm. Hay is digested by gut microbes and bacteria which generate heat during the process and give an 'inner glow'. A hungry horse is a cold horse and, because the horse's digestive system is geared to always having a little food passing constantly through it, a candidate for digestive disorder and discomfort.

Feeding little and often is, of course, one of the Golden Rules of feeding, yet the method so often used, particularly with stabled animals, of giving, say, three feeds, plus hay night and morning, is *not* little and often. It is erratic and leaves the horse for many hours with no food at all available, especially during the night. Dividing the concentrate ration, where fed, into four, five or even more smaller feeds spread over the twenty-four hours, maybe by means of an automatic feeder during the night, and giving *ad lib* hay except for an hour or two before work (unless that work is mainly walking) *does* constitute little and often, simulates nature and makes for more contented, physically comfortable horses less prone to indigestion and stable vices and able to work better. The even, constant energy supply also helps them to keep warmer, too, with no extra feed.

Apart from feeding little and often, a brief recap on the main principles of feeding might not go amiss.

Water before feeding is probably the next best-known adage. Horses who have water constantly with them in stable or field are less concerned with this aspect than those who have to be watered by being taken to water or having it brought to them at set times of day and then removed, which does happen in a few establishments. Horses in the wild normally drink morning and night, when possible, and simulating this method works well for domesticated ones too, where necessary. Also, horses eating grass obtain moisture from the grass plus rain water, dew etc.

Such horses should be watered away from enemies (at, say, a communal trough) who can put them off drinking. Horses normally take a long draught then raise their heads for a rest. At this point less knowledgeable handlers will pull them away thinking they have had their fill. In fact, they are probably taking a break. They will look round (looking for predators?) then lower their heads and take another long draught. Not until then have they drunk their fill. In fact, they will probably move away from the trough themselves when satisfied.

With bucket supplies (or water given in small plastic dustbins) the groom or owner can see just how much the horse is drinking, which is a guide to health. If automatic drinkers are used, try to use the kind with a meter so you can see how much or little the horse is drinking.

Making all changes in diet gradually rather than suddenly enables the gut microbes which digest the food to retain a healthy, fairly constant population, which makes for efficient digestion. Not all microbes can digest all food constituents, so if a new type of food is given there may be insufficient microbes to digest it and indigestion (colic) can result. If a food is suddenly cut out, conversely, the gut microbes will be starved and die off, again possibly causing indigestion. When new rations of familiar foods are received, they should initially be mixed with the old, especially hay, to ensure microbial adaptation, and when completely new foods are introduced they should be started with just a few ounces/grammes a day and very gradually built up over two or three weeks.

Using only good quality feed is common sense. The horse's digestive system is so sensitive that anything 'off' can cause colic.

Feeding something succulent (roots or hydroponic grass) every day to stabled horses often seems to be overlooked, yet it does help to satisfy the horse's natural craving for grass and other vegetation.

The need to feed according to temperament, work and weather has already been mentioned when discussing amounts. Temperament faults can often be traced to unsuitable feeding, and not just a reaction to too many oats but to mineral imbalance or deficiency and an unhealthy gut bacteria population. As in many general management matters, it is often well worthwhile consulting a veterinary surgeon or specialist horse nutritionist in such cases to obtain a properly formulated diet, maybe with a specific additive or supplement, to overcome the problem.

We are often told not to work fast or hard straight after feeding, particularly after a full concentrate feed. In the wild, horses grazing or browsing must often have been 'surprised' by a predator suddenly appearing and been forced to gallop off fast to survive. Also, horses grazing in a domestic paddock will suddenly kick up their heels and have a crazy few minutes, but such animals will have been 'trickle feeding', that is, putting just enough food through their stomachs and intestines to keep that specialised system working properly. A full concentrate feed is an artificial thing to them, so we must make no unreasonable demands in the way of work until time has been allowed for its digestion. Otherwise, the full stomach can press against heart and lungs and interfere with their functioning, and a working heart and lungs can, in turn, press against the stomach. Blood being used for digestion is diverted to the muscles, which need it for work, so incomplete digestion (resulting in colic) could result.

The final major point in feeding is that we are usually advised to keep to a regular routine and to feed at more or less the same times every day. In practice, it will be found that half an hour late or early, or even more, will not matter provided the horse has *ad lib* hay. He will not become too hungry (if at all) and will not gorge his other food when it arrives. Horses, whether in or out, only become fractious about feed times when kept on restricted diets, in my experience. Provided some hay is always available, if you miss the bus to the yard or your alarm clock fails to go off, it will not cause a disaster. Keeping to a *reasonable* routine, however, and not missing out a meal when the horse is away at a day's show, hunting etc., does make for consistent digestion.

The horse's food provides the fuel he needs to live and work on. Like a car engine, when fuel is used (or burned) up, waste products are created. Nutrients are carried in the bloodstream, absorbed from the intestines, to all parts of the body, either for immediate use or storage. The blood is also responsible for carrying away from the body tissues the waste products of metabolism. In a healthy horse correctly fed and managed, the waste products are easily coped with but if the horse is given too much food for the amount of exercise he is receiving, problems can arise.

In winter, many horses which are almost entirely stabled are on restricted exercise for various reasons: either their owners are working and do not have time to give quite enough exercise or there is a serious freeze which hampers the horse's work. In such cases, if the concentrates in a horse's diet are not immediately reduced but not entirely cut out, the excess nourishment and resulting waste products in the bloodstream can result in tissue damage, causing such things as laminitis, lymphangitis and azoturia (the latter when the horse starts work again).

All the above conditions are potentially serious so it is particularly important with stabled horses in winter to reduce concentrates immediately, and preferably before, there is a cut in work levels. Then, increase the work again when possible *before* increasing the concentrates. To keep the gut bacteria going, however, add, say, a single handful of the horse's usual concentrates to each feed rather than cut them out altogether.

The types of food available to you may vary according to the supply situation in your region, your budget and maybe what your horse will eat if he is a fussy feeder. Good hay, as mentioned, is an extremely valuable food in winter. Hay replacements such as silage, hayage and similar conserved, moist grass feeds and feeding straw such as oat straw and fodder straw, and barley straw at a pinch (combined barley straw which will have had the awns removed during harvesting), are all important in providing your horse with the essential roughage/bulk portion of his ration. Grass in winter has no appreciable feeding value even in a mild winter when it may keep on growing slowly, but roots such as carrots, apples, fodder beet if available, turnips, swedes and mangolds (if your horse will eat them) and soaked sugar beet pulp are good replacements. Concentrates include straight grains such as oats, barley (which can be fed bruised, cooked and flaked, extruded or micronised) and maize (fed in the same form as barley). The concentrate ration is also com-

monly given now as horse nuts or cubes of different energy/
protein levels according to the work your horse is doing, and
coarse mixes which consist of grain and other ingredients,
usually with a moistening or light binding agent such as oil or
molasses. Like cubes, they, too, come in different grades and
have the advantage that horses do not seem to sicken of them as
they often do if fed mainly cubes. However, buy smaller batches,
as they do not keep as well. Palatability is as important as
nutrient content: no food is any use if the horse will not eat it.

If the manufacturer's leaflet is studied, cubes and coarse
mixes have another advantage – they take the guesswork out of
formulating a ration. The owner simply feeds the recommended amount according to the horse's workload and type
and the balance of carbohydrates, fats, proteins, vitamins and
minerals takes care of itself. Such feeds are subject to strict
quality control, too, and the analysis is given on the label or
panel on the bag. Neither of these factors apply to straight
grains, some of which are very variable in quality.

Two other foods are bran and chop, sometimes called chaff.
Bran is the outer husk of the wheat grain, left after it has been
milled for human consumption. It used to be the 'thing' to
demand broad bran with large floury flakes, but since the
improvement of milling techniques and the craze for high-fibre
health foods for the human market, such bran is almost impossible to find. The flakes become smaller and smaller till the
bran resembles sawdust, yet still horse owners pay exorbitant
prices for it because it is a traditional food and 'you need it to
make mashes'.

It is, however, becoming more and more realised in the horse
world that bran is *not* an important horse food and too much of
it definitely causes bone disease (enlarged, porous, weakened
bone) because of its high phosphorus content. Horse diets need
more calcium than phosphorus, the normal recommended ratio
of calcium:phosphorus being $1 \cdot 1 : 1$ – always slightly more calcium than phosphorus. As many cereal grains are rather low in
calcium anyway, the addition of large amounts of bran to the
feeds upsets the ratio even more. If you do want to use bran,

maybe as a base for mixing in worming powders, pellets or other medicines, use as little as you can and certainly not more than one sixth by weight of the shorts ration, i.e. the concentrates/bran-type feeds as opposed to hay or hayage. That means that if you are feeding 3 lbs (1·3 kg) of oats or barley, do not add more than ½ lb (·2 kg) of bran.

Bran mashes are out of favour with nutritionists and many veterinary surgeons in the light of current knowledge on feeding horses stemming from research. They are usually recommended for sick, tired horses because it is said that they are palatable and tempt the appetite, being easy to eat and easy to digest. The exact opposite is true in both cases. Bran mashes are hard to digest (being largely fibre) and tasteless (which may be why so many books urge us to add a little salt to improve palatability!) and, as such, are hardly the sort of food you would wish to offer a sick or tired horse. Giving a bran mash once a week goes against one of the Golden Rules of feeding – make no sudden changes in the diet – calculated to upset a horse's digestion. Those three factors – difficulty in digestion, unpalatability and incorrect nutritional balance – are three very good reasons not to feed bran mashes and not to use any but small amounts of bran on a habitual basis, if that.

As hay and hay replacements have a higher calcium than phosphorus content, horses fed adequate or generous amounts of them will have a more nutritionally sound diet (all else being taken care of) than those on restricted roughage diets, particularly if fed high concentrate levels. Another way to correct the calcium:phosphorus ratio is to feed soaked sugar beet pulp regularly (a little in each feed) and/or dried grass meal, which is a constituent of most horse cubes anyway.

If you feel the need to give your horse a mash, instead of giving bran, give him dried grass meal thoroughly damped with soaked sugar beet pulp, which is a nutritionally sound meal, loved by most horses and easy to digest, especially if the horse is already used to them in his daily diet.

If you need to give your horse a low-energy diet, i.e. few or no concentrates, because the horse is off work for any reason, chop is a very useful foodstuff. It is simply hay and/or straw cut up short (about an inch/2·5 cm) and therefore has the same nutritional content of the materials from which it is made. As many animals may feel they are being done out of a 'proper meal' if fed only chop, various things can be done to brighten it up for them. A single handful of their usual concentrate can be added (which helps keep the gut microbes going, anyway) and molassine meal can be added, diluted black treacle or honey (if your horse likes the latter – some do not) or you could buy molassed chaff consisting of chop and molasses. The molasses, being sugar, does increase the energy content of the meal but not enough to cause problems. Soaked sugar beet pulp, particularly the kind containing molasses, can be added or coarsely grated or thinly sliced roots and fruit such as carrots and apples.

Many owners understandably want to feed their horses more 'warming' food in winter when the animals are exposed to the weather and letters often appear in the advice columns of horse magazines saying something like: 'Can you recommend a food for my horse which will give him more warmth without making him too energetic to ride? As foods like oats and maize are more heating than other foods, should I give him more of these?'

As all body processes, including maintaining body temperature, come from the energy in the *whole* diet, not just part of it, the best course of action would be to increase the energy content all round. If, say, more carbohydrate were added, this would provide a short-term boost in energy which might warm him up for three or four hours but then he would start to feel cold again.

In addition to giving a more or less constant supply of good hay or hayage, one good way to increase the energy content of the feed without the ill-effects of increasing the grain portion of the ration (hyperactivity, silliness, azoturia, laminitis, etc.) is to increase the oil or fat content of it. Fat provides two and a half times more energy than carbohydrate, so the diet is more 'energy dense' without cramming more concentrates, and their inevitable side-effects, into the horse. This is especially useful if the horse's appetite is not good.

This can be done by adding a teacupful of corn or soya oil a

1a A two-year-old Shetland pony: an ideal representative of the northern-horse type, with shortish legs in relation to size of barrel, rounded rib-cage, small nostrils and woolly coat hair.

1b This fit Thorough-bred event horse is a good example of the southern-horse type, with his more oval-shaped barrel, longer legs in relation to body size, larger nostrils and finer hair.

2a The thick, dense coat of northern-horse types insulates them very effectively against harsh winter weather.

2b Although he does not have the benefit of a thick coat, this clipped, working horse is in well-covered condition for the winter. He is, in fact, carrying a little too much condition for hard work (compare him with the fit Thoroughbred event horse in Plate 1b).

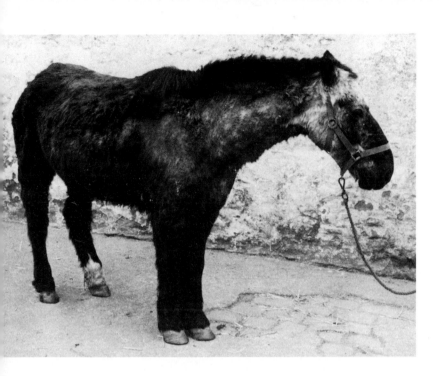

top
3a Even native ponies need feeding! Hardy though they may be, lack of food and a winter of exposure can result in this sort of condition. This twenty-year-old pony, photographed when recently taken in by the Horses and Ponies Protection Association late one winter, had suffered both.

bottom
3b It's surprising what good feeding can do! This is the same old, neglected pony after a few months of correct care and feeding.

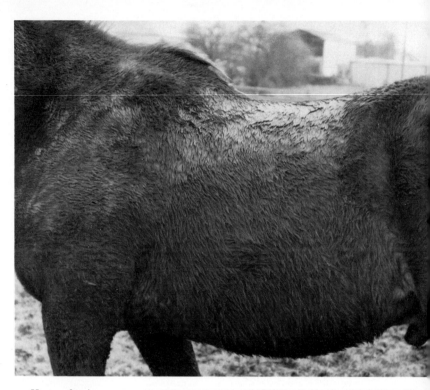

4a Horses often infuriate their owners when they roll in mud, but they do it for a good reason. Apart from discouraging skin parasites, when the mud dries on, it forms solid protection against cold winds.

4b Although we tend to think of horses at grass as living in natural conditions, in fact there is no shelter at all for them in an open type of landscape with conventional fencing like this.

5a A beautiful job! A properly trimmed and laid hedge that will provide a significant windbreak and a strong barrier fence for many years to come. Such hedges require little maintenance once completed, trimming every two years or so being all that will be necessary for several years. (*Crown Copyright*)

5b Although not laid, this hedge is high and fairly dense, thus helping considerably to lessen the force of the wind. It has been allowed to grow higher to provide extra shelter.

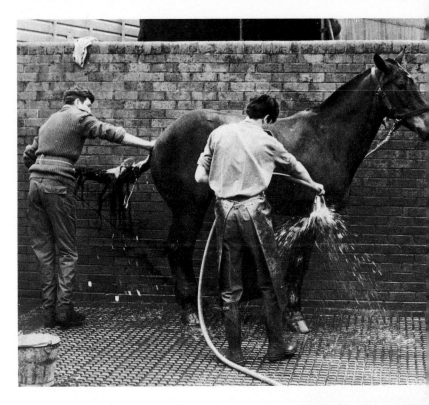

6a Washing down horses in winter as a quick way to remove mud after work is standard practice in many military establishments. (*Clive Hiles*)

6b If the job is done quickly and the horse kept well covered with plenty of clothing, there is no harm in washing dirty horses in winter. In fact, some people find it quite relaxing! Here, the horse's body and neck are well covered with an anti-sweat rug and woollen rugs, drying off while his legs are done. Note his plaited tail, which keeps the hairs cleaner, protects them from wear and breaking and prevents bits of bedding clinging to them.

7a Two high quality rugs available from Hydrophane Laboratories, both with correct shaping and cross-surcingles. On the left is a New Zealand rug and on the right a quilted stable rug.

7b Lungeing a horse in his New Zealand rug is one stage in accustoming him to the feel of straps in unusual places. This is a well-shaped canvas rug lined with wool. Note the good fit: it comes well in front of the withers, not on top of them, and well back just past the root of the tail. It also comes below the bottom line of the belly, so helping to shield that area from wind. Extra-deep rugs are also available.

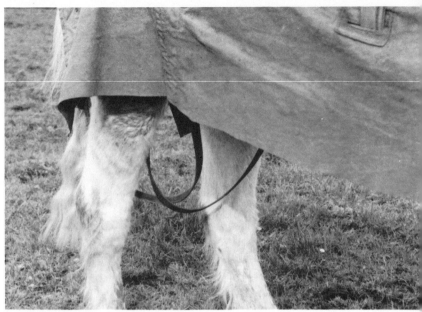

8a These leg straps
are dangerously long.

8b Link the straps through each other
so that they hold themselves away from
the sensitive skin inside the horse's
thighs.

8c There should be
just this much play in
correctly adjusted leg
straps.

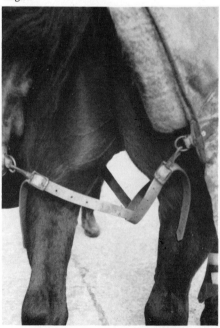

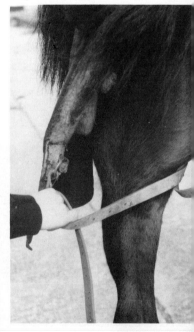

day, by feeding boiled linseed (which, however, is also high in protein, which can cause problematic side-effects) or up to a tablespoon a day of linseed oil. The latter should obviously be that obtained from feed merchants for animal food and not the sort sold by do-it-yourself shops to home decorators for cleaning brushes and which is highly poisonous! Obviously, in accordance with the rules of good feeding, the addition of extra oil should be done gradually over, say, two weeks.

Even though their warming effect may be short-lived, warm, cooked feeds have the same physical and psychological effect on a horse as they do on us, and for that reason alone are worthwhile.

Any feed can be warmed up by damping it with black treacle diluted with very hot water and thoroughly mixing it up. For something a little more substantial, try boiling linseed with pearl barley and blackstrap molasses and adding it to a normal feed on a cold night. As these ingredients will add significantly to the energy and protein content of the original feed, it is a good idea, especially with stabled horses, to reduce the concentrate part of the feed by, say, 2 lbs (1 kg).

Soak half a teacupful of linseed in a large pan of water (half a gallon or two litres) overnight. An hour before the appropriate feed, add 1 lb (·4 kg) of pearl barley or whole barley grains, with more cold water if necessary, and bring it to the boil, watching carefully to see that it does not boil over. Boil it hard for 20 minutes, adding a large tablespoon of thick, blackstrap molasses as it heats up, stirring occasionally. Then add this mixture to the feed (it will be enough for two horses) and allow to cool, if necessary (it probably will not be). I have found that most horses raise the roof for this particular recipe. There is no need to let it stand and 'cook' as you are not making a conventional mash, simply offering a warm feed on a cold night.

Boiled barley is another way to give a warm feed, although in the amounts normally used I doubt whether it would have the effect of putting on condition as the old books say. Simply take whatever amount you require and put it in a large sieve on a pan of boiling water. Stir it round and over occasionally so the rising steam penetrates all the grains, and when they are all swollen and softened, they are ready to be mixed with an ordinary feed, taking the place of the same amount of concentrates, but feed daily or you could upset the digestion.

Obviously, any of the above hot mixtures can simply be stirred into a 'false' feed of chop, perhaps a little bran and/or dried grass meal.

Even in winter, except perhaps the mildest when grass may still grow slowly, the advantages of giving succulents (roots/ fruit) to horses, particularly those mainly stabled, should not be overlooked. Most horses really appreciate them. Carrots and apples, coarsely grated or thinly sliced, are usually the favourites, but some animals like a whole turnip left in their manger to scrape and crunch on at their leisure, particularly at night. About 5 lbs (2·2 kg) is a reasonable daily amount.

A clipped, stabled horse in winter will probably need more food than that same horse doing identical work in summer, as he will still be using up more energy to cope with the cold. His clothing, put on to replace his long winter coat, will not compensate for the colder weather. Those who say that their animals' winter rations, when in work, are far different from summer may be overlooking the fact that their horses could well be under-exercised at this time of year. They perhaps forget, or discount the value of, turning out and its beneficial effects on mind and body, and the fact that in warm, especially hot, weather, horses and humans alike often feel less energetic than in cooler, fresher weather. A horse needs 10–20 per cent more food for each 10 °F (5·5 °C) drop in still-air temperature below freezing, and more if wind chill is present.

All animals carry body fat as well as flesh, even the most emaciated, although in their case the amounts will be very small. Fat is a good insulator and it is normally a good plan to have your working, and particularly your resting, horse go into the winter carrying a little more fat than in summer. It may be difficult, unless the horse is an exceptionally good doer with a super-efficient digestive system, to put weight on a skinny horse in winter. Obviously, horses in strenuous work such as racing or hard hunting, should not carry too much fat because of the unnecessary strain of carrying it around during work, as applies to any athlete, along with the weight of the rider and perhaps dead weight, too, in the form of extra lead. A good range of clothing for the stable, exercise and when and if turned out will help to ward off the cold for such a horse.

In late spring and early summer, most horse owners and managers are keeping an eagle eye on potential hay crops and, therefore, their forthcoming winter supplies. After a good season, hay will probably still be readily available, if slightly more expensive than at other times, towards the end of winter. In a bad year, though, the price of hay is often double for the same product what it was in October by the time February, and particularly March and April, come round. Transferring allegiance to hayage products often does not solve the problem as they, too, are made of the same basic product, grass. In times of shortage, feed dried alfalfa, dried grass, chop and sugar beet.

Often, conservatively minded horse people feel obliged to pay highly inflated prices for almost any hay they can get, when its nutritional value could just as easily be created much more cheaply by buying in other forms of bulk and roughage to keep the horses not only well fed but entertained and occupied, as hay does.

The best plan, apart from looking ahead as much as possible and buying in as much good hay as you can store, is to scout round for whatever nice hay you can get at a reasonable price, and then buy whatever else of good quality you can find, such as clean oat straw, barley straw, cattle fodder straw, hayage products and maybe silage. Then tell a vet or nutritionist what you have been able to get and ask him or her to work out the proportions of each you should feed daily to give your horse a resulting balanced roughage portion of his diet.

It may also be advised that you feed a higher fibre coarse mix or cube, and up the amount of roots to 10 lbs (4·5 kg) daily to add bulk. Remember, roots are mainly water anyway, and roughage. What water your horse takes in with his roots he will simply not drink, so do not worry about the commonly heard complaint that roots will 'fill him up with water'. He only wants and needs so much water, anyway.

The remainder of the dietary requirements can be made up with concentrates so that your horse ends up with a properly balanced diet made up of a wide range of roughage/bulk products. When feeding poor quality (but clean) hay, or more or less any straw, the protein requirement will be lacking, so you will probably need to feed a higher protein concentrate portion of the diet, or simply a protein supplement, as advised.

Incidentally, it is impossible accurately to balance a diet by eye and feed tables, but the body can compensate to some extent with a minor imbalance. To ensure precision it will be necessary to have each sample of feed analysed by a laboratory. This is not so expensive as you might imagine and will only have to be done once as long as your present supplies from a single source last. The specialist working out your diet will arrange analysis, if required.

Feed supplements and additives of all kinds fill saddlers' and feed merchants' shelves, to the bewilderment of most of us, and very tempting advertisements lead us to believe that only *this* product is worth buying and that, in fact, our horse can barely survive without it! In truth, many of these sometimes expensive products are unnecessary and others could do harm, even when fed according to the manufacturer's instructions, should your horse's diet already be balanced, as they can *un*balance it. Similarly, his deficiency, if any, may not be the one covered by the product you are thinking of. Again, expert advice should be taken before adding any supplement willy nilly to his diet.

From the point of view of winter feeding, substances which will probably be needed are folic acid, choline, lysine, methionine and biotin. The fat-soluble vitamins A, D, E and probably K will almost certainly need supplementing during the second half of the winter (after Christmas in the northern hemisphere) as, although the body can store them, supplies will be used up by that time and cereal diets will not be adequate to provide them.

The advantages of a perhaps higher-than-normal fat content

in the diet also extend to keeping the skin and coat, and also the hooves, in good condition during the winter. When feeding extra fat/oil, the results can often be seen in the coat as the oil builds up over a period of a very few weeks. In fact, if slightly too much is fed, it can be a *dis*advantage in this respect because excess grease in the coat flattens it and reduces the hairs' ability to trap between them the all-important insulating layer of air. A close watch should be kept and if the coat appears to be becoming greasy as opposed to naturally lustrous, cut back on the oil content a little. Then the amount should be sufficient to enhance the suppleness and, most important, water-repellant qualities of your horse's protection against the outside world without going too far and reducing his natural insulation against the cold.

The B vitamins choline and biotin and the amino acid methionine are also important in maintaining the good condition of skin, hair and horn. What is good for one is usually good for the others, and both biotin and methionine have been reported as helping considerably in improving the quality of hoof horn in horses with previously poor feet. Feet are crucial at any time of year. In winter, especially if horses are exposed to wet ground conditions for many hours a day, horn can soften, weaken and rot or wear away easily. A supplement containing appropriate amounts of these two substances could well be an advantage, if your consultant advises it.

There is no way to avoid expenditure on feed in winter; whether the horse is in or out, working or resting, he will need feeding, whereas if he is on reasonable grazing in summer all you probably need pay is its rent, and if the land is your own it will be almost free apart from the cost of its care. There are, however, various ways to economise and, just as important, to ensure that you are not caught out with no hay or paying through the nose for whatever supplies you need.

It is worthwhile financially consulting your vet or nutritionist again to find out if your horse's dietary needs could be met with a mix of different ingredients from those you are thinking of using. If you normally feed oats, for instance, and they are going to become prohibitively expensive this winter, a mix of other ingredients could provide the same dietary requirements at much less cost, but it does take expertise to work it out and get it right.

If storage space is your problem, particularly for hay and hayage, although it sounds unlikely, it is often worth renting extra storage space, buying in bulk at cheaper prices, at the cheapest time of year, too (normally summer), and avoiding the extortionate prices which will almost certainly appertain in late winter and early spring. You will not only probably save money in the long run but actually ensure that you do have supplies when other people are scratching desperately around trying to buy anything at any price. You could even make a profit selling your excess hay!

But maybe you do not have enough spare cash to buy several tons of hay. Again, because of the rapid and high price rises in fodder towards the end of winter and late spring (they can often more than double in a few weeks), consider taking out an overdraft at the bank. Yes, it really can be cheaper to pay the interest on an overdraft than to pay those awful prices which may get you in the end if you do not.

It is quite feasible to keep hay and straw outdoors if you have no storage space. Hayage, of course, usually comes in polythene bales, often double skinned, and can easily be stored outdoors, but as rain ruins hay and straw, it must be protected from wet. Rigging up a raised floor of planks and bricks (high enough for a cat to get underneath to reduce habitat for rats) and covering the hay with a tarpaulin weighted down with old car tyres is probably the most practical and the cheapest way to stop water getting in. On dry days, remove the cover when possible to keep air circulating. Using polythene is quite common but can cause problems with the hay 'sweating' unless it is frequently aerated, which can be a nuisance. Before you press into use your own and friends' garages for storing hay and straw, check with your local fire authority as it may not be allowed within a certain distance of residential premises.

Normal steps to prevent wastage should obviously be taken.

Do not feed roughage loose in muddy, windy fields as it will be blown away or trampled in; use haynets or proper racks in the field shelter. Do not tip concentrates direct on to the ground but use a container – even a plastic washing up bowl is better than nothing. If the horse is the type to tip his food out, use a travelling manger which can be hooked on to the fence or fit a corner manger in the shelter with bars across the corners to stop him scooping the food out with his nose.

Do not buy *crushed* grain in larger quantities than you can use within two weeks as it will by then start to deteriorate to the extent that it may not be fit to use. The best yards crush their own oats daily, which, however, is impractical for many small establishments. Store concentrates in galvanised bins, if possible, as rats can even gnaw through plastic dustbins. Keep them cool (no problem in winter) and dry. Also, do weigh concentrate rations to avoid over-feeding, which is not only wasteful but causes the usual results of over-feeding already mentioned – and a possibly expensive vet's bill to follow.

Working out how much a particular diet is going to cost is quite easy, yet few people seem to bother doing so. You will know how much per ton (or tonne) or per 25-kg sack a particular food costs. For the latter simply divide the cost by 25 to get the price per kilo and multiply that by the daily (or weekly) amount your horse will be eating. You and your nutritionist/vet can easily work out the price of your intended diet that way and maybe come up with a cheaper but nutritionally equivalent diet. However, if the horse finds it unpalatable and will not eat it, it will be far more expensive than the original diet would have been.

The body of a mature horse is about 70 per cent water, that of a young one even more. Water is even more vital to life than food in that a horse can live for weeks without food but for only days without water. Water is needed in most body processes. The blood is largely water and so is lymph, the fluid of the 'supplementary' circulatory system. Digestive juices are fluid and so is mare's milk. Urine and sweat, both important in excreting waste products from the body, and the latter in temperature control, are both almost entirely water. In fact, the whole body is bathed in fluid which can only exist if the horse's water intake is sufficient.

We hear a good deal about dehydration in summer, particularly when horses perform endurance-type work (long-distance riding, eventing or driving trials) but tend not to think about it in winter. However, it can occur sometimes.

It is a horse's natural tendency not to drink so much in winter and many of them seem to drink very minimal amounts. This is thought to be one of nature's devices to retain heat. The blood 'thickens' slightly and so is able to retain heat more easily, and the fluids surrounding the body's cells are not so abundant for the same reason. (One only has to think of a water-filled central-heating radiator to realise how effective water is at transporting and releasing heat.) Horses who drink too little in winter could be both underfed and cold; therefore check the diet and clothing. In pastured horses in winter lack of water is a major cause of colic due to frozen water sources.

Although most horses are their own best judges as to how much water they need, the odd one will actually become dehydrated. This can also occur if the horse is not drinking enough for any other reason. If he is turned out, perhaps the approach to his watering point is so muddy or rutted that he puts off facing it until he is desperate. If his container, in stable or field, holds any ice at all, this is enough to put some horses off drinking enough, if at all. Others will not drink if the water is not quite clean, if other horses are scaring them away from the source, if they distrust the container and so on.

If all the above points have been taken care of and the horse is still drinking too little, apart from taking veterinary advice on a chronically dehydrated horse there are ways of increasing his water intake.

Firstly, the amount of roots in his diet can be increased to 10 lbs (4·5 kg) daily with advantage. Secondly, try warming his water slightly, either with a heater kit or manually before offering it to him. Although drinking very cold water does not really appear to have any serious consequences, particularly if the horse is not overheated, most horses *will* drink more if it is a more comfortable temperature, not exactly warm but not very cold either. Offering tasty drinks like old-fashioned oatmeal gruel, the water in which sugar beet pulp has been soaked and linseed tea all help to get fluid inside the horse.

Linseed tea is simply boiled linseed, using about twice as much (or more) water, and oatmeal gruel is made by creaming about a cupful of oatmeal (ordinary porridge oats) with cold water, then topping it up with boiling water and allowing it to stand, covered, till cool enough to drink. Most horses love it while it is still warm.

Because inadequate water intake has so many adverse effects, among them poor appetite and constipation, every effort should be made to check that the horse *is* drinking properly, and to encourage him to do so more freely if not. The simple dehydration test of pinching up a fold of skin on the shoulder or neck and seeing how long it takes to fall back down (it should be almost immediate) should be carried out daily, as a warning precaution.

It may also be necessary to give an electrolyte supplement, as these body salts are lost in dehydration. Electrolytes are needed for enzyme activity, enzymes themselves being proteins which act as catalysts, increasing the rate of biochemical reactions in the body. In other words, they are essential to life's processes. As ever, do not just add a supplement (available in powder or syrup form from saddlers) unless you know it is needed; your vet will advise you on this. Some horses will not take supplements in their water, but try a different brand and keep a salt lick available at all times in field and stable.

Opinions seem to vary as to whether drinking very cold water is detrimental to the horse or not. In his stable management classic *Stable Management and Exercise*, Capt. Horace Hayes says he witnessed horses in Russia drinking very cold water while hot from work and coming to no harm. In another book, more generally famous, Anna Sewell's *Black Beauty*, there is the famous description of how Beauty became very ill after being given cold water when hot from work. This scene may or may not have been written from the author's personal experience, and may have perpetuated the belief in the horse world that giving cold water to a hot horse is dangerous.

Some veterinary surgeons advise against it, but others feel that it may actually help to cool the centre of the body. What they all agree on is that water should be given in small amounts (about a litre) until the horse cools down, whether the water is cold or not. If the horse is already cool, water just above freezing would do no harm at all, of course, although, as already mentioned, horses do definitely drink more if the water is nearer blood heat or even about 20 °C (68 °F) – what is generally loosely regarded as 'room temperature'.

Finally, horses require an average of 12 gallons (54·4 litres) of water daily, so every effort should be made to ensure that they are drinking freely in cold weather. There is a common misconception that horses, and particularly native ponies, can get their water needs from eating snow in winter. A horse would have to eat from 50 to 70 gallons (roughly 227 to 318 litres) of snow to obtain his water requirements. It is very unlikely that a horse would do this, and even so, eating snow seriously chills the body. Although feral horses have been known to survive severe weather by eating snow, the risk to their well-being is tremendous, and not the sort of situation we should wish to impose on domesticated horses.

5 Care of the Skin and Coat

The structure and functions of the horse's skin and coat were discussed in Chapter 2, particularly in relation to their role in temperature regulation. The skin is a much under-rated organ: it is as vital to life as any of the other main organs because of its several roles. Humans and animals suffering extensive burns often die because of its destruction and its care could probably receive a good deal more attention than it does. Although skin diseases do occur, a well-cared-for, well-fed horse's skin usually remains in such good health that we tend not to think about skin problems until they happen.

In winter, particularly for horses exposed to the weather, temperature maintenance and waterproofing are two functions of the skin and coat which are more vital than ever. All horses and ponies grow a winter coat but those 'hot'-blooded, southern types grow a comparatively short, thin one which is nothing like enough protection against a temperate or sub-arctic zone winter. Northern types, however, such as the British native Mountain and Moorland ponies and cobs, Icelandic Ponies and Haflingers, are well equipped to withstand such winters if in good health.

It is good health which maintains the condition of skin and coat. No amount of proprietary coat dressings will compensate for the bad effects of parasite infestation, unnatural over-exposure to the elements or a poor diet (see Chapter 4).

The summer coat starts casting about August and a little of the winter coat will grow, then more summer coat comes out and more winter coat grows, until by about November the full winter coat is set (in the northern hemisphere). Northern-type animals often have a so-called 'double coat' in winter, sporting a soft, almost downy underlayer which considerably increases the insulating effect of the longer, more dense, winter coat. Such breeds also often have in their coats at intervals long drain or cat hairs mostly down the flanks and under the jaw and, of course, have varying amounts of hair (called 'feather' when heavy) on the legs.

The hair does not grow indiscriminately but in streams or swathes to aid drainage of water, the most noticeable 'drainage channels', apart from the back of the fetlocks, being at the hip, down the quarters and down the flanks.

Coat colour in animals plays various roles, the most important being camouflage. Although our domesticated horses and ponies have long lost this need – and, indeed, lost their original innate colouring due to being repeatedly cross-bred by man – colour can give us, their carers, an idea of how well an animal is likely to respond to the elements. There are many old wives' tales about colour, but the fact is that melanin, the colouring agent present in the skin which determines what colour a horse's coat will be, does have a strengthening effect on the skin.

Animals with large white patches and white socks and stockings, under which there is colourless pink skin, succumb much more readily to rain rash and mud fever on their white areas and to sunburn and photosensitisation (often seen on nitrogen-rich pastures) in summer. Chestnut horses, too, seem rather susceptible to the effects of the weather.

It is the horse's natural tendency to undergo a slight thickening of the skin in winter, with a view to heat retention, accompanied by a slight receding of the blood capillaries in the outermost layer of skin, the epidermis, the very top layer of which is composed of dead skin cells which flake off continually and which are removed by wind, rain, rolling and grooming.

The skin's natural lubricant, sebum, is secreted from glands in the skin and creates a thin layer of oil on the skin and hairs which protects them from friction and water to some extent and helps with insulation. It also helps to deter bacteria and fungal infections. When horses roll, however, grains of soil and grit cling to the sebum coating. Opinions vary as to why horses roll, but as they do it, given a choice, in soft ground when hot and when first turned out, it almost certainly helps them to dry off and gives them a protective coating of soil, sand or whatever to help ward off parasites such as lice. A dried-on coating of mud certainly protects them against wind.

The skin of a healthy outdoor horse functions perfectly. It does not become excessively clogged with dandruff, grease and mud because these are constantly being removed by rain and wind. Good health helps the horse to resist skin diseases and the effects of parasites, although, as in all fairly naturally living animals, parasitism and disease do occur as part of the balance of nature.

We may feel that a horse looks better clipped and shampooed but both these practices are obviously highly artificial, even shampooing: although a horse in nature will be rained on, he does not have oil-stripping soap applied. We can, however, work *with* nature to our advantage in controlling the growth of coat hair. The same techniques as were detailed in Chapter 1 regarding bringing mares and stallions into breeding condition apply to coat control. If we keep the horse warm, expose him to light, feed him well and clothe him (again for warmth), we can 'kid' his coat into thinking it is summer and *vice versa*.

Because good skin and coat condition are so important to maintaining health and in temperature control (which, in winter, is mostly keeping warm), keeping up the coat's appearance will inevitably help in those functions. There are various branded coat dressings available which give a gloss to the hair and which would help to condition the hair of a horse in generally poor condition, but the real evidence of condition shown by a naturally shiny, soft coat and supple, elastic skin comes from inner good health. Many such dressings can also cause skin reactions in sensitive horses.

Chapter 4 has already given details of feeding appropriate for winter and explained the value of a higher oil/fat content to the diet at this time of year, not least for its effect on the skin and coat. Prevention of coat wear is also a factor, not only for appearance's sake but because worn, rubbed hair means less protection for that area and is a forerunner of sore, maybe raw, skin, meaning pain for the horse and an easy inlet for infection. A daily watch should be kept for rubs or thickened areas which could mean that the skin is being subjected to friction or pressure from clothing or tack. It is difficult completely to avoid rubs from clothing during a long winter, but the fact remains that if clothing *is* rubbing, it is simply because it does not fit properly (see Chapter 6).

With the stabled horse, daily grooming obviously helps to maintain appearance and condition. Although it is not essential thoroughly to body brush and strap a stabled horse every single day, the horse will certainly appreciate the stimulating effect of the dandy brush (used gently on thin-skinned horses) and the refreshing sponging part of the grooming routine. Full grooming should be done daily if at all possible. The excess dandruff forms a breeding ground for parasites, being organic matter, so should not be allowed to build up; with stabled animals, there is no regular rain, or the facility to roll in what we call dirt but which to the horse is a substance which helps to keep his skin healthy. Establishments which provide a sand pit for their stabled horses to enjoy a roll, particularly after work, are providing physical satisfaction and enjoyment and mental pleasure for their horses, even if the sand *is* groomed out afterwards.

If, for any reason, a stabled horse is allowed to become very dirty, a good way to remove the excess dandruff and grease is to give the horse a thorough, but careful, going over with a plastic-toothed curry comb, especially if it has a winter coat. This really gets down to the skin and loosens caked-in dirt without scratching. If this is followed up by a vacuum grooming or at least a thorough hand grooming of the conventional sort, albeit with some effort, the dirt can be removed.

Basic grooming techniques include picking out the feet, dandying off dried mud, sweat and manure, body brushing to push the bristles down to the skin of a clipped horse and remove excess dandruff and grease, and, perhaps, wisping (sometimes called banging) which, like any grooming, stimulates the skin and helps to spread the sebum over it and down the hairs for maximum lubrication and protection.

Out-wintered horses, if wearing waterproof rugs most of the time, should be occasionally vacuumed, if possible, to remove the build-up of dandruff which cannot be washed away. Body brushing is hardly effective on a long winter coat but should be done occasionally as thoroughly as possible if there is no vacuum groomer available.

Horses without rugs should be watched carefully for skin condition and should receive the minimum coat grooming. Eyes and feet, especially, should receive daily attention, mud should be sponged from the sheath/udder area and the dock should be sponged at least every few days, but great care must be taken to dry off sponged areas properly (the sponge should only be damp, anyway) to prevent chapped skin. Old towels are best for this. The horses' coats should be dandied two or three times a week, depending on their condition and remembering that, if the horses are resting, the plastering of mud they give themselves will help to protect against wind and there is certainly no need to remove it daily. Fat being a good insulator, whatever grease *is* allowed to build up will help to some extent against wind and wet.

Working, out-wintered horses can be a problem as, unless rugged up, they will invariably be filthy (in our eyes) when wanted for work. The normal procedure of thatching them with straw or an anti-sweat rug under an old, ordinary rug, can be used to dry them off, so that mud can be thoroughly removed before tacking or harnessing up. Putting tack on top of mud will certainly cause a very sore skin. Strictly speaking, it is only the areas touched by tack that need to be groomed before exercise, although you may feel embarrassed riding or driving an otherwise muddy horse.

If the horse is simply wet, there is nothing wrong with scraping off the worst of the wet and tacking up with an absorbent numnah (quilted cotton being ideal – not synthetic fabrics, which are not absorbent) and using an absorbent girth such as lampwick or mohair. The horse will probably sweat to some extent during work and become wet under his tack anyway, so drying him off beforehand is a waste of time.

If you do not have time to wait for a wet, muddy horse to dry by thatching and you do not have a special drying box or heat lamp in a stable, again it is quite permissible, and not at all harmful, in my experience, to hose off mud from critical areas (saddle and girth) – really thoroughly – scrape off excess water with a sweat scraper, give a good rub with straw or old towels, and tack up with absorbent numnah and girth. Muddy heads are more difficult to cope with for fear of getting water in the eyes and upsetting the horse, but mud *can* be sponged off here and the head carefully dried with old towels before putting on the bridle. Putting a bridle on top of mud, although undesirable, is not likely to result in the sores caused by mud under saddles or driving harness because of the lack of pressure and weight. Obviously, it is much better to allow time for the mud to dry on the head (and back) and brush it off, if at all possible. A thatched, woolly-coated horse can take two hours to dry thoroughly.

There are all sorts of taboos given against washing down horses in winter, but it normally causes no trouble if the horse is thoroughly dried afterwards or kept on the move in clothing, and the job is done quickly. It is standard practice in many military, police, hunting and racing stables, and, bearing in mind the above provisos, is certainly the best way of dealing with mud, whether the horse is clipped or not.

Sensitive-skinned horses can be made quite sore by constant brushing off of gritty mud and although the back and loins can be thatched, and the legs bandaged over wet mud, what about the belly, which receives so much mud kicked up during work? I have known several horses become chapped and sore on the relatively thin, sensitive belly/sheath area due to their owners or managers believing that it is better to allow the mud to dry on and brush it off later. Mud fever (dealt with more fully in Chapters 7 and 10) is not confined to the legs!

Mud can simply be hosed off with cold water and horses do not seem to mind. I do feel, though, that in very cold weather it must feel better for them if slightly warm water is used, and this is certainly an advantage when actually shampooing, as it does remove grease better.

It is a definite boon to have both hot and cold water available in a yard, either in a tap outside or in a special washing/drying/clipping box. A mixer tap, so that warm water can be directed through the hose, is not expensive and can be installed by any competent handyman or do-it-yourself expert. Sponging off the mud with warm water is an alternative but it is more time consuming and not as thorough as a good hosing down. Treating yourself to proper facilities pays dividends at a time of year which is difficult enough anyway.

An old reason for not using warm water is that it is supposed to open up the pores of the skin, enabling soil and particularly clay grains to become trapped in them. I have always felt this to be rather far-fetched and have never personally had any problem. If a horse is hot (as opposed to slightly warm), cold water would probably be detrimental, especially if used on muscle-mass areas such as quarters and loins, when it might cause too sudden a chill and resultant muscle cramps.

A decent hosepipe, with a screw fitting which screws firmly on to a complementary tap fitting, is another big advantage and obviates having to clamp the hose to the tap – and its flying off during use, frightening horses and fraying tempers.

Another simple item of equipment which is worth its weight in gold is a hand-held home hairdryer. Horses soon get used to them, and they are particularly useful for drying off vulnerable areas such as belly, heels, pasterns and lower legs. The same precautions are needed as with any electrical machine (groomer, clipper, etc.) – keep the flex out of the horse's way and make sure everything is properly earthed. Wear rubber boots or rubber-soled shoes just in case.

New on the British market at the time of writing is a horse-drying device called the Trocken-Max. It consists of a PVC laminated body and belly cover to which is connected a hose running to an electric motor. A stream of warm air passes along the hose, lifting up the cover so that it floats around the horse's body. The German makers say it has been tested extensively and claim that without exception, horses behave quietly and calmly during drying.

The too-frequent use of soap and shampoos on the coat does strip it of too much natural oil. If a horse is washed fairly frequently, soap is certainly not needed every time – in fact, it is only needed if the coat is significantly greasy or when removing oil-based creams which may have been used in the prevention or treatment of rain rash or mud fever. Clear water, including rainwater, removes quite a lot of grease and dirt from the coat and skin.

There are various categories of horse which are bathed regularly, even daily, all year round, among them harness racers. The process is quite safe if a few common-sense rules are followed.

First, you need somewhere completely draught-free, preferably a proper washing box or at least somewhere very sheltered where you can tie your horse, preferably on hard standing. Even a large car port will do, depending on the wind direction at 'bathtime'. Second, you will need at least two and preferably three or more rugs and/or blankets to cover the horse from ears to tail. British readers will find the American-style coolers, which do just this, a real boon. They are available in several good British saddlers now, often by mail order and particularly, of course, in those stores selling western riding equipment. Treat yourself to two woollen ones if you possibly can, along with two cooler clamps. These are like giant clothes pegs which hold the coolers together under neck and belly. Large office bulldog clips will do as well.

Next, if you do not have warm running water in your yard, you will need at least three large buckets of hand-hot or at least warm water. Inexpensive water heaters can easily be rigged up near any tack-room sink which will provide the water; otherwise buy a large electric kettle. You will also need two large sponges, shampoo of your choice or mild washing-up liquid if required, a sweat scraper (although you could use the sides of your hands) and a few old towels. An anti-sweat rug and/or straw for thatching will also be an advantage.

Tie up the horse, with a haynet, and have everything to hand to avoid delays once the horse is wet. First, starting behind the ears, wet the horse's neck and body all over with warm water and one of the sponges. Leave the legs and tail but include the mane. Next, if using shampoo, apply it to the other sponge and, using quick circular movements, soap the horse thoroughly all over the wet areas. Now go back to your remaining two clear buckets of water and clean sponge and thoroughly rinse off all the soap, especially from the belly and in the roots of the mane and underneath it (this is where you will wish you had a hose if you have not got one). Finally, scrape the horse all over to get off surplus water.

Now put on the two coolers, *both* of them, especially if it is a cold rather than a mild day. If you have straw and/or an anti-sweat rug, you can put these on first, although they are not essential. Clip the coolers together under the neck and sheath area to muffle up the horse and prevent cold air from getting in. Now you can do his legs and tail, and the head if you wish, although many people do not wash heads. You have to be extra careful not to get soap or water in the eyes and ears.

With the towels you can dry the head, the legs, particularly heels and behind the pasterns, and the dock and between the buttocks. Bandage the legs over cotton wool, gamgee tissue, knitted dishcloths or even less comfortable straw or hay, to help them to dry off.

Now remove the clamps and feel under the coolers. The horse will be warm and drying off nicely. If you have not used straw or an anti-sweat rug, periodically rub him down under the coolers with the towels. Obviously, he can be back in his own stable now.

You will probably notice droplets of water forming on the top of the coolers as the moisture rises and evaporates away. This also shows that the advice so often given to put an ordinary rug on inside out over thatch, turning it the right way up when the horse is dry is risky, at the least. While the horse is drying out, the top of the rug is the lining. This then becomes damp with rising moisture, and is put next to the horse when the rug is later put on the right way. Even on top of a blanket, the rug is damp and will probably strike through. If using ordinary rugs rather than coolers, it is better to use an old rug or make one out of empty feed sacks (see Chapter 6).

If you have no coolers, use normal towels, rugs and blankets to keep him swathed and muffled up, with bulldog clips if necessary, including on his neck which is a source of considerable heat loss.

Obviously, once the horse is completely dry you can rug him up normally, but if he usually goes out, wait a few hours before putting him back in his field, probably with a New Zealand or other waterproof rug on.

Another method you can use to bath your horse if your acilities are not draught-free, though one which is slightly more inconvenient, is simply to do one area at a time. First wash and rinse the neck, mane and shoulders, scrape and perhaps rub them down with a towel, then cover them with a bath sheet, rug or blanket while you do the back, sides and belly, then cover them, too, and finish with the loins, quarters, flanks and thighs. Finally, cover those areas and do the tail and legs.

Thatching with straw or an anti-sweat rug is not essential with any method but does speed up the process. An unthatched horse will take a good half hour longer to dry than a thatched one, depending on the length of coat. To prevent thatch or sweat-rug marks staying in the newly washed coat, remove the straw or mesh rug while the horse is still very slightly damp and rug up normally as this will straighten and flatten the hair and the horse will certainly come to no harm. If you want to rug up again later with another dry rug, it will probably make you feel better but is not essential!

If you cannot bring yourself to wet your horse during the winter, and many people understandably cannot, particularly if facilities are not too good, try cleaning your horse with the hot towel method.

You will still need water-heating facilities of some kind because you will need a large bucket of very hot water, a good thick terry towel, a dash of washing up liquid if the horse is very greasy, rubber gloves for yourself and human or animal hair conditioner if his coat is dry or out of condition.

Soak the towel in the water (containing either shampoo or conditioner, if required), wring it out thoroughly and lay it on the horse's coat, starting with the neck, allowing the heat to penetrate for a couple of seconds, then rub the hair in a circular movement until the towel starts to cool down. Simply repeat this process all over the horse, folding back the rug and blankets to do each area as you reach it. For the legs, wrap them, one at a time, in the hot towel and rub briskly up and down. Rub well under mane and forelock and, lock by lock, get down to the roots of the mane; also separate the tail hairs on the dock to clean there. You can wash the tail normally or do it lock by lock with the towel.

If one 'heating' is not enough for any particular area, simply repeat the process until it comes acceptably clean. You can also do the head, inside the nostrils and between the hind legs and buttocks with this method.

I feel that many more yards could install heat lamps in at least one box to make life easier in winter for drying off shampooed, hosed-down horses and also those wet from rain. Heat lamps at present cost about £30 and run for a very few pence per hour. The heat is not excessive but just enough to make a cold, wet horse feel comfortably warm, and to dry him off in an hour (for a long coat) or less. They certainly save time, effort and possible worry, particularly if a horse is cold, or has been washed with cold water. Do not, however, use them on horses wearing the modern heat-retaining rugs, otherwise you could virtually 'cook' your horse, or at least cause blistering or seriously overheated skin.

Horses should always be brought in from exercise cool, of course, but we have all known circumstances when due to either temperament problems or rain (when we may have been trotting home on purpose to keep the horse warm) the horse comes in less than cool. If the horse is actually hot, he should be walked round in a light sheet over an anti-sweat rug, or with the rug folded back at the withers, to cool down considerably first. A warm horse can be stabled with such clothing and not be in danger of chilling too fast. If he is actually cold, however, do thatch him with straw, if available, or put one or two anti-sweat rugs on with a couple of ordinary rugs and/or blankets on top. Clip a towel or blanket on his neck, too, bandage his legs and dry belly, heels and the backs of pasterns thoroughly with towels and/or a hairdryer. The object is to get him warm and dry quickly.

Clipping is something nearly all horse owners are familiar with in winter. Its advantages, as mentioned elsewhere, are ease of grooming, quickness of drying off and the ability to work without losing (by sweating) too much condition. Obviously, a clipped horse will chill much more than a long-coated one if left standing around. Clipping also reduces the time a horse can spend outdoors in the field and increases the amount of food needed in cold weather.

I feel many people clip more extensively and more often than is necessary – or than is beneficial to the horse's well-being. A little less fetish about 'smartness' would probably lead to a more comfortable horse. Very few horses need clipping all out or hunter clipping except possibly those with naturally very long, greasy coats, and then only if in hard to strenuous work.

Blanket clips, particularly high, short ones (a little higher up the sides and taken back to the front of the saddle) are plenty for practically any other horse. They take the hair off the parts where the horse sweats most (neck, shoulders and breast) and gets dirtiest (underneath) so do all the jobs needed of a clip, yet the horse retains that vital protection over his vulnerable back, loins and quarters.

Trace clips are ideal for a horse, pony or cob in light to medium work. They are also ideal for horses who are turned out a good deal (with a rug in wet or windy weather), as the top of the body, including the head, as well as the legs are left unclipped, so offering protection. In a 'chaser' clip, the head hair is also removed. Many steeplechasers and similar horses race with this clip perfectly satisfactorily and it makes me wonder why a more extensive clip is ever felt necessary for most horses.

An Irish clip is like a trace clip but also leaves the hair on round the top of the hind legs, again, even more suitable for outdoor horses who stand with their quarters to the weather, as they have full protection there.

Well-bred, fine-coated horses in light work often manage with a gullet-and-breast clip, sometimes called a pony clip, in which the hair is clipped off the breast and underside of the neck, or even just one or two clipper-head widths up the gullet and maybe under the jaw. This clip is suitable for ponies in light work out most or all the time.

If you are a working owner with restricted time to ride during the winter you may be willing to sacrifice energetic work at weekends in exchange for the convenience of not having to clip your horse at all. I say convenience because, in those circumstances, you can save considerable time on exercising if you can turn your horse out, even if only for a couple of hours, during the week, and this may be more acceptable if he is not clipped at all. Also, it will save on food and clothing if he is not clipped and he will feel more comfortable when out.

Alternatives to clipping are to let the horse go the whole hog and grow his full-density, natural coat and work very little, or to restrict the full growth by clothing the horse as soon as he starts to show significant signs of growing the winter coat. As most horses start to cast the summer coat in August, you can start by putting a summer sheet on him at night then, graduating to a light rug as September arrives, worn all the time provided the weather is not so mild that it makes the horse uncomfortably warm. Gradually progress to a heavier rug and/or an under-rug or blanket, the idea being to fool the horse's brain into thinking that it is still warm weather and there is no need to grow an unduly long, thick coat. You could also turn him out in a light-weight New Zealand rug, progressing to a heavier one later on, and exercise him in clothing, to the same ends. You will end up with a short winter coat which will be fully set by the end of November at the latest and may well find that you can work your horse more and keep him fitter despite not having clipped him, although obviously not to the extent that you could had you clipped. This 'shortened' winter coat also makes body brushing an unclipped stabled horse quite practicable, and, indeed, necessary if reasonable cleanliness is to be maintained.

When the horse is turned out, he can wear a turn-out rug of some kind so he does not start feeling the cold and sprouting a significantly long winter coat (although the coat may grow a little more until January) and will still have protection hair on his underneath should he lie down in the mud. Horses do prefer dry lying areas but these may be impossible to find in winter except in the shelter. Clipped horses then often suffer from sore, chapped skin, if not actual infection (mud fever) because the very areas that touch the mud have no protection, a point often overlooked by those who, say, trace clip an animal, give it a New Zealand rug and feel it can winter out without harm. It might – but probably only if it has somewhere dry to lie down.

In spring, the full winter coat will start to cast probably a little earlier than in a clipped horse, and can be helped by vigorous grooming, rubber curry combing and so on. Remember, though, that if you get rid of the winter coat too quickly, while the weather is still chilly, the summer coat may well come through rather longer than you wanted, particularly in horses born early in the year who often seem to cast and set their coats earlier in the relevant season.

Using the above techniques to avoid clipping is also, of course, an ideal way of avoiding hassle with a horse who is difficult to clip, either through fear, temperament or sheer dislike. Some might call it the coward's way out, others would quote that 'discretion is the better part of valour'!

If you feel that clipping is essential but do have a difficult horse, there are various steps you can take to help to improve matters. Probably the least troublesome, if most expensive, is to get your vet to give a sedative. Modern sedatives are much more predictable and reliable than older types, and some are much shorter acting – by the time the clipper is nearing the end, the horse is just coming round, but not to the extent that it starts playing up.

Twitching the horse, which releases into the bloodstream the body's own sedatives, endorphins, due to pressure on the top lip – an acupressure point – can be done by a traditional rope twitch (the handle of which can be stuck up the side of the headcollar if you are alone), an improvised twitch made by means of binder twine on a hoofpick handle, or the popularly titled 'humane twitch', of which there are various types, all operating on the principle of a clamp fitted to the top lip. These are reckoned to have less risk of damaging the skin than a perhaps too-tightly applied twitch. The twitch should be periodically moved – twitched – to have the best effect and, like a sedative, usually takes a little while to work, several seconds in any case. The twitch should be removed every few minutes, the top lip rubbed, and the horse given a little rest, maybe while you clean the blades or let the clipper head cool down, before applying it again. Twitching is not really appropriate for a time-consuming, extensive clip.

If it is the noise of the machine which frightens the horse, try buying one of the quieter general animal clippers now available, particularly those for dogs. The clipper heads are not quite as wide but they are so very much quieter. You could also try stuffing the horse's ears with cotton wool, playing the radio or singing, all to disguise the noise. Accustoming the horse to the noise of electric machines such as clippers, groomers and hair-dryers before the Great Day does help.

Some horses object to the pull of the clipper on the skin and this can often be overcome by using the rotary-type electric groomer on the horse beforehand to accustom him to it, as the brush head has the same effect.

If the horse becomes only mildly agitated, a simple form of restraint such as holding up a foreleg often does the trick. In any event, turning the event into a battle will simply compound the problem for the future. If you can get the horse to associate clipping with something pleasant by being kind to him and letting him eat something he likes during the process, such as good hay interspersed with a tasty feed and someone giving him fruit or mints, plus much praise, he will improve noticeably.

It is a good idea not to try to do too much at once with a tricky horse, but do the job in, say, two stages if necessary. Also, do everything possible to avoid discomfort – the blades should be as sharp as possible, correctly tensioned according to the instructions (a slow speed is usually best to start with), and do not wait for the blades to become hot and clogged before you clean and cool them or, apart from the uncomfortably warm metal, you will be pulling and tearing the hairs which will obviously hurt. The horse should be as clean and dry as possible before starting, again to avoid pulling. If the horse starts to sweat up during the process, you might as well stop.

Try to pick a mild day so that the loss of coat will not be too much of a shock to your horse, and have plenty of rugs and blankets to throw over him as his natural protection falls off.

If you decide to buy your own clippers rather than pay someone else to do the job, you will be spoilt for choice as to type and make. Watch the equestrian press for advertisements (and for detailed articles on how to clip, which never fail to resurface in horse magazines every autumn!). There are cool-running clippers, quiet-running clippers, cordless, battery-operated clippers and hand-operated hairdresser-type clippers for very difficult horses and tricky places such as the head and ears. You will also need a circuit breaker in addition to seeing that the plug is properly earthed – a belt-and-braces operation but well worthwhile.

Try to have the horse on a dry, rubber matting-covered floor, particularly if he is shod, wear rubber boots yourself, have good lighting and keep the cord well out of the way. Remove water buckets from the stable (empty automatic waterers) and if you need an extension lead, the connection from the transducer to the mains should be off the floor even if it is dry; pile it into an empty rubber or plastic stable bucket or similar container preferably without a metal handle. Check that the cables are in safe, covered condition.

Let the clippers run for a little while to accustom the horse to the noise. If you anticipate trouble, before even doing this brush the horse with one hand and gently stroke him with the (unplugged) clippers in the other. Then, when they are running, put a hand flat on his shoulders and press the running clipper body on your hand to accustom him to the vibration. Gently start clipping at a place unlikely to cause much trouble and which will not be a disaster should you have to give up before finishing. The shoulder and breast are usually good places. When possible, use firm, long strokes, not leaning on the clipper or pushing it but almost letting it take itself along against the way the hair grows. For tricky places like the elbows, get an assistant to pull the horse's leg forwards to smooth out the skin; this is easier than trying to smooth it out yourself.

As clipping progresses, get someone to body brush the clipped areas if possible to get rid of the hairs and any possible grease and dandruff revealed by the clipping process. The hot-towel technique described earlier is good for cleaning off a newly-clipped horse and helps get rid of that just-clipped look.

Every five minutes, or less, during clipping, run the clipper blades in a bowl of methylated spirits or surgical spirit to clean them, then oil with a light oil (do not let oil or spirit get into the ventilation holes on the clipper body). This also helps to cool them down and is quicker than brushing the hair off the blades. If you are doing a fairly extensive clip, you may need a few spare pairs of sharp blades on standby. Trying to clip with blades that are less than sharp is one of the easiest ways to make a horse difficult; the next easiest is to keep clipping when the clipper head has become too warm. Nicking the horse, even if you do not draw blood, obviously hurts and you only need one painful cut to create long-lasting problems with some horses. Have some antiseptic handy to dab on just in case.

Clipping machines are expensive items: it pays to keep them clean, well oiled and serviced.

Obviously, clothing appropriate to the amount of coat you have clipped off and the horse's constitution should now be provided. Probably a slight increase in food will be needed immediately but it is better to leave it at that and see how the horse goes rather than to risk the considerable side-effects of over-feeding concentrates.

Whether horses are clipped or unclipped, careful trimming makes a vast difference to their appearance. Even out-wintered horses can stand a certain amount of trimming to the benefit of their appearance.

Even in animals who, for showing reasons, need ostensibly untrimmed manes, forelocks and tails, judicious tidying up can be done if well disguised. Manes and forelocks can be shortened by snapping off long, straggly ends between thumb and forefinger and likewise with the tail. A longish mane does help to retain some heat in cold conditions, but if the mane is required to be plaited in the conventional way, it will need to be about 4 ins to 5 ins (10 cm to 12 cm) long at the most and the same for the forelock. If you do wish to leave the mane long but wish to plait on occasions, your problem can be solved by a crest plait.

Tastes vary as regards how to treat tails. Pulled tails are still very common but more and more horses and ponies seem to be making public appearances of all kinds with their tails plaited instead of pulled. For horses who spend long hours outdoors, either in the field or working, particularly at slower paces, an unpulled tail is a definite advantage in heat retention. American research has shown that in two control groups of horses of similar types kept in similar conditions, those with pulled tails lost up to 20 per cent more body condition (weight) than those with unpulled tails when fed identical diets. Even when the diet energy content of the horses with pulled tails was increased, they did not do as well as their naturally equipped colleagues. The heat loss, as described earlier, from the area between the buttocks and thighs can be considerable and to protect these parts from the weather when horses adopt their instinctive tail-to-the-weather stance in bad weather, tails should be left full, and plaited for special occasions.

The length of the tail over the ages has been the subject of fashion. These days it is generally considered 'right' for a horse to have the bottom of his tail, when in action, about 2 ins or so (5 cm) below the point of his hocks. When standing, this will bring it probably about half way down his cannons. Especially in winter, there is no advantage in a longer tail than this as it can easily become clogged and balled up with snow and mud. In summer, a slightly longer tail is an advantage in swishing away flies.

In a horse with good (as opposed to fuzzy, wiry) tail hair, I think nothing looks nicer than a full, racehorse-type tail with a clean bang across the bottom, particularly if the hair is straight and glossy. Horses with wavy hair at the tops of their tails would, I feel, look smarter with the tail plaited for special occasions than left loose – again, just personal taste.

More bones of contention arise over trimming legs and heels. The hair was put there for a purpose, some say – protection against wet and mud – but that same hair holds *in* wet and mud (particularly the lather) and excludes air. These conditions are perfect for the mud fever bacteria to thrive. The skin is weakened by the wet and maybe scratched and irritated by the gritty mud, and bacteria find it easy to get a hold. Also, 'hairy legs', except in native breeds, are not liked. Long fetlock and lower-leg hair also makes it difficult to care for the legs as regards the prevention of mud fever.

Some animals seem able to stand all day in oozing mud and never get mud fever; others only need a short hack down the lane and flare up within hours. With susceptible animals (who will probably be unable to live out completely), I have found the best way is to trim (but not necessarily clip) heels and lower legs, rinse off mud, dry thoroughly and rub in liquid paraffin as a preventative. I do not subscribe to the school which says allow the mud to dry on and then brush it off, because experience has proved to me that this is the way to allow the bacteria to become established and also to cause irritation to the skin when brushing and picking it off.

Clipped legs do not look attractive anyway. They are better trimmed with curved fetlock scissors and comb, combing up against the lie of the hair and snipping off the hair to your desired length. The hair up the back of the cannon and over the coronet can be trimmed the same way for a neat appearance on unclipped legs.

A hairy head can really spoil the most elegant horse's appearance, but for the horse's sake it is better to compromise between shearing him of his essential 'antennae' whiskers around muzzle and eyes (which sadly is so common) and leaving the head *au naturel*. The ears should not have the inner hair removed as this protects against rain, excessive cold draughts and wind and helps to prevent debris falling down inside the ears. However, the slightly longer tufts at the base of the ears can certainly be trimmed off. Simply close the edges of the ears together and snip off with scissors any hair which protrudes beyond the edges, which will include the hair at the base.

The sometimes long hairs (even in finely bred horses) along the underside of the jaw probably spoil a horse's appearance more than any others. Again intended as drain hairs, they are probably better left for horses out all the time, although I have never had any problems arise through trimming them off with scissors and comb.

A useful and readily available trimming tool which is not usually to be found in tack stores is a razor comb. This makes for quick and really easy trimming of just about any hair except body hair. They are normally available from even the smallest chemist's shop and simply consist of two rows of teeth with a sharp razor between them, set slightly down from the ends of the teeth. As you comb the hair, it is trimmed at the same time.

You can use a razor comb for thinning long manes by combing from underneath at the roots – excellent for horses who simply will not tolerate having their manes pulled – for shortening long manes by combing the ends at the length you want them (hold the ends taut in one hand and comb with the other from on top), for trimming fetlocks, coronets, cannons and jaws by simply combing the hair up the wrong way, and shortening over-long but essentially natural tails by using in the same way as for a long mane. With a little practice they produce a really smooth, natural look and are well worth having around.

Pet shops are also treasure troves of trimming tools to make your job easier, as they stock all sorts of dog-trimming devices which are just as useful for a rather larger four-legged friend. Thinning scissors (with a comb on one side and a scissor blade on the other) are not so useful, however, as they inevitably cut the hair at different lengths. They *do* thin out a thick mane, for example, but the resultant different lengths of hair left do make subsequent plaiting rather difficult!

6 Clothing

Despite the horse's excellent protection of skin and coat, with their major role in temperature regulation, there are times in domesticated conditions when a good, basic range of quality, well-fitting clothing is a definite advantage, if not a necessity, to horse and owner in winter.

As discussed previously, the maintenance of body temperature is critical to the maintenance of life itself. The skin, with the nerve endings, sweat glands and capillaries it contains, sends messages to the brain as to whether the ambient temperature is too warm or too cold, helps to cool down the body by means of the evaporation of sweat and by the contraction and dilation of blood vessels and houses the hair follicles of the coat, which itself plays a considerable and vital role in temperature regulation. It also protects the skin from friction, among other things.

In winter, the layer of warm air trapped between the hairs of the thicker coat in an unclipped horse is vitally important in keeping the horse warm. Obviously, clipping removes this protective, insulating layer and the more extensive the clip, the colder the horse feels. Clothing does help to replace the hair when the horse is not working, and comfortable, well-fitting clothing helps the horse to feel good, just as it does his owner.

On the other hand, unsuitable clothing, the wrong size and badly designed, can do as much harm as good, if not more. It annoys the horse and so puts him under unnecessary stress and anxiety, it probably causes the quite common vice of rug tearing, it causes painful skin abrasions, fistulous withers due to

9a An exercise sheet or ordinary rug used for exercise purposes is turned back and secured under the girth, like this.

9b With horses not used to being exercised in clothing, walk them round at home first to accustom them to it. Always use a fillet string, adjusted to the correct length like this one, to prevent the rug from blowing up and frightening the horse.

10a Badly poached and waterlogged conditions like this in a gateway are, of course, common in winter. Even just walking through this to a drier area is enough to give susceptible horses mud fever. It is well worth excavating areas like this and laying sand over bricks or rubble. Used bedding from the stables can also be put to good use on such areas, if laid thickly and regularly.

10b Opinions vary as to the best way to prevent mud fever. It is the author's experience that the most effective way is thoroughly to rinse off mud . . .

10c . . . and equally thoroughly to dry the legs afterwards. After removing excess wet with a towel, the quickest way to dry the legs is by means of a hair dryer, bandaging afterwards. All electrical appliances should be properly earthed and a circuit breaker used as an extra precaution.

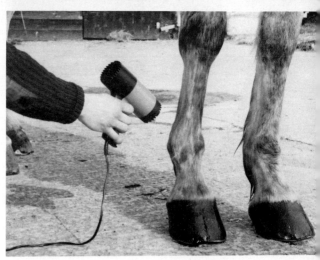

11a Bedding of all kinds (here it is barley straw) should be well banked up for extra warmth, including behind the door.

11b Shredded paper (in this case Diceabed) is a warm bed in winter, and especially appropriate for horses with respiratory disorders (the author prefers a deeper bed than this). As a matter of safety, a rug just thrown over a horse without a roller, like this, should have the front breast strap left undone so that if the rug slips round it will fall off completely and not remain hanging round the horse's neck.

12a Ride-and-lead is a good way to make the most of the daylight hours, provided your horses are used to it and road conditions are suitable in your area. Pass the nearside rein through the offside bit ring . . .

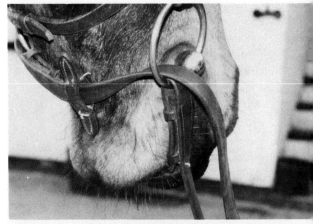

12b . . . and tie a knot in the end of the led horse's reins, which you should hold with both hands.

12c Train the horses in the yard before venturing out.

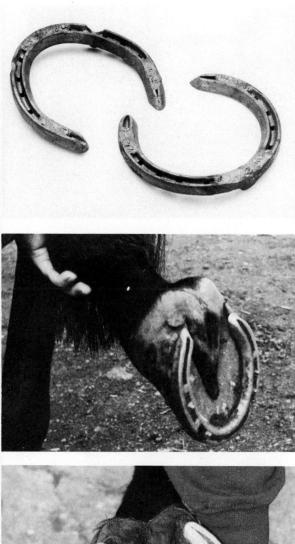

13a These are Sure-grip shoes, available through your farrier or direct from CSB Fabrication, Loughter Mill, Newnham Estate, Plympton, Plymouth, Devon PL7 5BH. They are treated with borium on the toes and heels. Depending on the way in which the horse wears the shoe, it can be placed anywhere on the shoe in the fullering, on request. Sure-grip are excellent shoes for roadwork, giving good roadholding and long-lasting wear, enabling them to be removed, the feet trimmed, and the shoes reset. Borium wears rough with use, not smooth like some hardeners.

13b Four small road studs in a pony's hind shoes, for extra grip.

13c An ordinary modern hunter shoe, fullered and concaved out, with pencilled heels.

14a What's the quickest way to deal with muddy harness and bridles? Do what the Army do and throw it in a tank of water. (*Clive Hiles*)

14b Allowing stabled horses time to graze in hand each day if they cannot be turned out breaks the monotony and gives them a little of their natural food, grass, which they still look forward to even in winter when it has little feed value. (*Peter R. Sweet*)

15a Horses and ponies do not mind cold, still weather at all and will nibble down through the snow to find grass. (*Pony/Horse and Rider*)

15b A ten-month-old foal experiences her first snowstorm. She has quickly learned to turn her quarters to the weather. (*Kicksports for Pony/Horse and Rider*)

16a A thin horse is a cold horse, and it can be difficult to put weight on an animal in winter. The dip in front of the withers and the prominent hip-bones are clear signs of lack of condition under the winter coat.

16b The same horse from the back, showing 'poverty lines' down the quarters. The full tail helps to protect the horse from driving rain and wind.

pressure there, maybe dead or decaying skin if the matter is not put right, excess grease and dandruff if too much clothing is worn and can trip and badly injure horses if it does not stay put. If 'staying put' means being strapped up in a straitjacket, this in itself causes great discomfort and irritation both mental and physical.

Some people do go to extremes and grossly over-rug their horses. This causes discomfort from the possible weight of the clothing, skin inflammation, hair loss and overheating. Then, when the horse goes out, even if wearing exercise clothing, he can become chilled easily if doing slow work on a cold day.

For years, the Americans were far ahead of the British in their attitudes to clothing, and their famous Baker blanket was indispensible to them but regarded by those 'Brits' who had never experienced it as something of a curiosity. How on earth did it stay on, for one thing? It has no surcingle or roller! It is *bound* to come off and cause an accident, we would think, despite the years of successful use proving otherwise. And those strange crossed straps under the belly! Whatever do they do? No, it is not for us. We will stick to our good old jute night rugs and woollen day rugs and keep them on with strong, padded rollers.

But in the 1960s a quiet revolution took place in the British horse world. Ultra-conservative as the British are, it was slow to take off, but the change which was started by the now equally famous Lavenham quilted nylon rug (albeit with an elasticated surcingle on the early styles) has gone on apace and it seems to me that jute and woollen rugs are now in a minority as more and more owners give their horses the advantage of correctly, comfortably styled, lightweight clothing, the latest stage in the revolution being the introduction of thermal textiles and 'breatheable' fabrics which allow body moisture to evaporate up through the fabric but prevent rain from getting in. (To be fair, the Gannex rug, an offspring of the famous Gannex mac, was the first breatheable rug available a good twenty years ago, but it never really seemed to catch on, despite being very efficient.)

Nowadays, the terms 'night rug' and 'day rug' have largely gone out of use, as all-purpose 'stable rugs' of synthetic fabrics of all kinds take their place. Of course, there *are* still jute night rugs and woollen day rugs in use, and no one would deny that the latter do give that look of luxury for special occasions. (Incidentally, there are some firms who continue to make them but with modern crossed surcingles rather than a single attached surcingle round the girth or a separate padded roller.)

As far as waterproof rugs for turning out are concerned, the original New Zealand, first sold here as the Emston, is still very much around. In natural canvas lined with wool, it was the first experience many British owners had of a properly shaped and fitted rug. It has a back seam which undulates to fit the spine – up for the withers, down for the back, up for the croup and down again towards the root of the tail. This particular rug also has a drawstring inside the back edge of the rug over the root of the tail which can be adjusted for a personal, snug but not tight fit. There are large darts at elbow and stifle to take up the usual slack material there, which simply flaps about, lets in cold air and, because it is obviously not contoured to fit the horse's body, prevents the vital self-adjusting quality of any well-designed rug which keeps it in place *without* those awful, constricting 'round-the-girth' surcingles and rollers. The rug has leg straps which fasten around the hind legs to keep the back end in place, and two breast straps at the front. All these features combine to create correct fit, superior design and much more comfort for the horse.

The Australian rug is also very good but not so well known here. Instead of hind leg straps, it has front leg straps which come under the belly, and a fillet strap behind the thighs.

Modern turn-out rugs (almost universally called New Zealand whether or not the makers are entitled to use that designation) are made of various synthetic materials with equally varied methods of waterproofing them. Both front and hind leg straps are available, crossed under-the-belly surcingles and, on some of the best makes, specially designed, sometimes even colour-coded, harnesses to ensure safety and security provided they are correctly adjusted and fastened. It has to be admitted that a common error with owners/grooms is to fit New Zealand leg straps too long, with the result that some horses have managed to get both hind legs down one 'hole' and have been seriously injured as a result.

Neck hoods are an item of clothing which complement turn-out rugs and do prevent excessive heat loss from the neck; presumably they feel to the horse like polo necks or turned-up collars to us. Many clothing manufacturers make them to attach to their turn-out rugs round the neckline.

Woollen blankets for under-rugs are still in use; they are also available in synthetics such as acrilan. However, many of the modern rug makers produce properly shaped under-rugs in all sorts of materials such as fleece and thermal fabrics. Some clip in and others, apparently miraculously, stay put under their top rug without being attached, simply fastening at the breast – again, the value of proper shaping and fabrics which mould to the body come to the fore.

The synthetic fabrics themselves are very varied. Nylon is very much still with us but is not of the breatheable variety of fabric. The latter have the advantage that they can be put on a horse wet with rain or sweat without needing an anti-sweat rug or straw thatch under them, and the moisture rises up through them.

One make, the Quorn, is filled with polystyrene beads which appear to create a beneficial negative electrical charge and seem not only to encourage the excess moisture and dirt out of the coat but are said by users to have helped horses stiff from arthritis, rheumatism or sheer old age.

When a horse is clipped, the belly is nearly always clipped and therefore exposed. This is quite a large area from which heat can escape but one which is usually left unclothed. One make of rug currently available, however, the Rohan, solves this problem by having a wraparound style. The usual areas are covered but there is a wide swathe of material which also goes under the belly, from elbows almost to the stifles, and between the forelegs.

The linings and fillings of synthetic rugs vary from brushed nylon or cotton to synthetic, hollow fibres and various thermal materials. The range is very wide and expanding all the time. The choice is certainly not as easy as it was in the days when all the choice we had was woollen day rugs, woollen under-blankets and jute night rugs unlined, half-lined or fully lined with wool.

The great advantage of most synthetic fabrics is their warmth, with lightness plus easy laundering. You can machine wash and dry one within a few hours. Some fabrics, and particularly fillings, however, cannot stand hot water or to be tumbled dry at a high temperature, as they melt into a solid, useless mass.

In addition to traditional canvas New Zealand (and similar) rugs, there are lightweight waterproof sheets suitable for turning out in wet but mild weather, or for keeping an unclipped horse reasonably clean for riding.

Boots and bandages have not escaped the clothing revolution. Woollen stable bandages still seem the most popular, with crepe bandages for exercising. However, various plastic and PVC boots are available, some fleece-lined and with hook or clip fasteners rather than straps and buckles. These can be easily washed in warm soapy water and dry much quicker than the old box-cloth or felt boots, and obviate soaping and oiling leather ones.

So, whatever kind of rug an owner wants for his or her horse, there is certainly no longer any need to buy the bad, old-fashioned type, usually cut in a straight line down the back seam and secured by a surcingle or roller around the horse's girth. The modern ones, with correct shaping and crossed surcingles or leg straps/harnesses are so much more comfortable for the horse and easier work for us. The arch or anti-cast roller is likely to give the horse a jab on the back muscles each time he lies down and tries to roll, possibly bruising him in the very place where the saddle goes – a fairly sure way of giving a horse a sore back. Rollers and surcingles, either from this sort of thing or from sheer pressure, even when padded, were and are probably responsible for many more sore backs and 'cold-backed' horses than is generally imagined.

Combined with good design must go good fit. Whatever type of rug you decide on, the basic elements of good fit remain the same. First, the rug must come *in front* of the withers, not on top of them as is so very often seen. It must fit snugly round the base of the neck when fastened at the front, yet you must be able easily to slide the flat of your hand round inside the neckline. There must be no pull whatsoever on the points of the shoulders.

In depth, most rugs are too short. They should come below the elbow and stifle; the horse's belly must not be visible below the bottom edge. Some designs of rug, for stable or field, are described as 'extra deep', and are that few inches/centimetres longer to prevent draughts or cold air too easily reaching the clipped belly area.

At the back, the back edge at the spine seam must just cover the root of the tail. Some good rugs do this, but are then extended round the buttocks for extra warmth, being kept in place either by their leg straps, which, of course, fasten on the back edge, or by a short fillet string. There should be no pull on the croup or the points of the hips. Turn-out rugs of all kinds should be slightly roomier than stable rugs, and extend a few inches beyond the root of the tail at the back.

Rugs intended for grazing horses need care when being fastened at the front. Some say that the top strap must be a hole (or an inch/two centimetres) tighter than the bottom strap to prevent the rug slipping back too easily. However, for grazing, this strap could well be slightly looser than the bottom strap as the horse has to get his head down in comfort without pulling the rug on his withers (which should not anyway be a problem if the front half of the rug fits properly).

The main causes of rubbed hair and bald, even sore patches are poor design and wrong fit. Some horses with very fine coats and skin are more subject to rubbing than others, but strictly speaking, if the rug fits properly these problems just do not happen. Meanwhile, until a properly fitting rug can be found, lining the areas which rub (usually round the neck and on the shoulders) with various materials does help, and bald patches can be lessened by rubbing into such areas a little baby oil. Lining materials include real sheepskin, silk (old headscarves), polyester skirt lining (or, again, old headscarves) and even plastic fertiliser sacks or dustbin liners, though I have always had more success with natural fabrics than artificial ones, some of which are, in practice, quite rough and harsh.

Apart from badly designed and fitting rugs, a very common sight is filthy ones. Some yards seem to feel it quite normal to wash rugs every few months rather than every few weeks or even days, depending on the equine wearer's personal habits. Dirty rugs and blankets cause itchy, inflamed and possibly diseased skin and with today's synthetics there is no need, or excuse, for making a horse stand in grubby clothing.

Rugs are expensive, and the horse needs a spare while his main one is being laundered (which only takes a day with most synthetic ones). However, even if you only have one, you can easily make an emergency top covering which will do for a few hours, or can be used when thatching to keep the main rug dry, out of hessian or jute feed sacks, if available, or polyethylene ones. Simply open them out by slitting down one long side and the bottom seam, and sew two together, if necessary, to give yourself a piece of material about the same size and rectangular shape as a rug. Cut out the neck shaping, using your rug as a pattern, make holes for breast straps and other fastenings, and knot on binder twine in the appropriate places to keep the rug on for a few hours. Very much a Heath Robinson affair but much better than not being able to keep your proper clothing clean.

Old bedsheets, particularly flannelette, can be used for the same purpose or to make rug-shaped under-sheets. Placed next to the horse they are a boon at casting time as they do help to prevent the lining of your good rugs and blankets becoming coated in hairs, and are more comfortable for thin-skinned horses than some synthetic fabrics, or even wool.

Particularly with the type of rugs kept on with leg straps, and some crossed surcingles or other harnesses, some horses will need accustoming gradually to the feel of straps in strange places. First, put the rug on normally in a stable, having an assistant handy if possible. Fasten the straps *slightly* looser than normal and lead the horse round the box. If he does not object, lead him round the yard, progress to lungeing him or trotting him in hand, and finally turn him loose in, if available, a small paddock before putting him in his usual one.

Although synthetic clothing does not attract moths like that made of natural fibres, it can still hold disease-carrying dirt and pass skin infections from one horse to another if shared. Most of it can be washed in a washing machine using hand-hot water and mild detergent, spun (or tumbled at a low temperature), and dried further simply by hanging out on a clothesline, over the fence or in any warm place. A warm tack room with an old-fashioned rack on a pulley is still a very useful facility in any yard. Nylon clothing can have the alarming rustle taken out of it by adding fabric conditioner to the final rinse, which in fact helps almost any fabric. Always follow the manufacturer's washing instructions.

Natural fabrics need more time and trouble. Woollen day rugs should be cleaned and the leather parts either removed first or thoroughly coated in Vaseline and oiled on return. Jute night rugs can be washed in a large washing machine or a bin in the yard with washing soda, which really removes stains. If they cannot be spun, hang them over a fence or gate to gradually dry out (they will probably break the washing line).

In all cases, really thorough rinsing is most important as even ordinary soap can cause sore skin if left in the fabric.

It is a great benefit to have a form of constant heating in the tack room, maybe by means of a thermostatically controlled device. It sounds a little extravagant but really helps to avoid mouldy, softened leather and general dampness in stored clothing. The room does not have to be actually warm; about 68 °F (20 °C) is enough to keep tack and clothing in good condition.

It is often recommended that moth balls be scattered among clothing (where appropriate) when storing it, but the smell is usually objectionable to horses and humans alike. I have found that putting a dash of TCP antiseptic in the final rinsing water does the same job without the unpleasant smell. Rugs and blankets should be stored in chests or drawers, preferably in plastic bags or wrapped in paper. Leather tack should be carefully cleaned and oiled, including metal parts, wrapped in rags and stored in a place which is neither hot, cold nor humid. Bridles should be undone and the individual parts laid flat. Saddles should be on proper supportive racks or stood on their pommels, and should be covered over with a large cloth, not plastic, which restricts air flow around the leather.

Waterproof turn-out rugs of all kinds obviously come in for rougher and dirtier treatment than any other. The synthetic ones can usually be machine-washed (check manufacturer's instructions) but may need periodical special reproofing treatment if repeatedly exposed to detergent. Even so, camping and outdoor shops, and many saddlers now, do sell good reproofers which do not leave a detectable coating on the fabric but effectively keep out water, although some need reapplying after each wash.

Canvas turn-out rugs are far too bulky and heavy for any machine readily available to most owners, but can still be adequately freshened up. If the leg straps are leather, clean them as you would any leather item. As for the rug itself, hang it up by the rings on its back edge (to which the leg-straps clip) on two strong, firmly fixed hooks on a wall, lining to the wall, and hose off the mud from the outside. Then spread it on a newly swept concrete or tarmac floor, lining up, and vacuum the woollen lining to get out as much dust and as many hairs as you can. If the lining is coated with hairs, dandy them off first.

The best way to vacuum the lining is to use a rotary brush type of suction cleaner and get two friends to stand with one leg on each of the two corners. They will hold the lining taut while you vacuum, and prevent the lining from getting caught in the brush. The suction-only type of vacuum is suitable for you to use by yourself but does not do such a good job.

Then, using lukewarm water, scrub the lining gently and

thoroughly with pure soap (baby soap or a mild medicated one will do). Next, hang it up by the rings again and thoroughly hose out *all* the soap, which may take a little while. If you can get some pressure on the jet of water it will help. Spread the rug, lining down, to drip, preferably over a hedge which allows plenty of air to circulate, or a fence. When it is less than sopping wet, turn it lining up to let the sun get at it, or put it in a warm place to dry out thoroughly. Finally, reproof the outer covering.

Because of the damp conditions in winter, special attention should be paid to stitching to check for rotting, particularly in clothing or tack not frequently used. Tack is particularly valuable and bodged up repairs reduce its value by more than an expert repair would have cost.

Clothing, too, can be expensive and although it is not usually a good plan to share clothing because of the spread of disease, particularly ringworm, to which horses seem to be quite susceptible (and which can, of course, be passed on to humans), money can be saved and perhaps the horse provided with an adequate wardrobe which its owner might not otherwise have been able to afford, by purchasing second-hand rugs and accessories. This plan can be quite effective provided the clothing is thoroughly washed and disinfected first.

Although it is possible for a competent saddler (look for the oval crest of the Society of Master Saddlers displayed on the premises and stationery) to remake a badly designed rug, if the work is extensive it could prove as economical to buy new. The back seam of any rug you buy should *not* be cut in a straight line but shaped to coincide with the undulations of your horse's back. Given this feature, the saddler could easily add darts at elbow and stifle to give the rug shaping if it has excess material there, and sew on either crossed surcingles, leg straps or whatever you prefer. If there is a single surcingle round the girth, have it taken off. Of course, if you are handy with needle and thread and/or a sewing machine, you could do this yourself.

Withers can be padded with sheepskin but a much better way of lifting the rug off this sensitive area is to sew inside the rug on either side of the seam (leaving a gap of about two or three inches, roughly six centimetres, between them), two pads of thick felt, the sort that old-fashioned children's pad saddles were made of. Each pad should be about six inches (fifteen centimetres) square and can be stitched in place with carpet or button thread, taking the needle in through the side of the pad so that the stitching does not touch and possibly rub the horse.

This same treatment can be given to poorly designed New Zealand rugs with a surcingle and, probably, a straight spine seam. (It is better not to have the surcingle at all as it prevents the rug readjusting to the correct position as the horse moves around. Once it has slipped it stays slipped!) The saddler should be able to cover the surcingle slots in the sides to make them waterproof but if, for any reason, this is not possible, the rug can be made suitable for use by leaving it as it is and sewing two more felt pads to the rug lining directly under where the surcingle goes over the spine. These four pads together will 'wedge' the rug in place on each side of the withers/spine and not only keep it on much better but remove any pressure at all along the backbone, making the rug acceptably comfortable for the horse.

Owners should check daily for any signs of rubbed hair, developing bald patches, raised, thickened skin or heat, swelling or soreness, all of which are signs of clothing rubbing. The most usually affected areas are the withers, points of shoulders, spine (if an ordinary single surcingle is used), croup and points of the hips. All these things can be prevented if, quite simply, the rug fits properly.

Because horses are not so susceptible to the cold as we are, we tend perhaps not really to check whether they are warm enough, particularly in wet and/or windy/draughty conditions. Whether the horse is stabled or out, the same basic guidelines apply.

The tell-tale areas are ears, belly in front of the stifles and loins. Feel the horse with your bare hands. Start with the ears and, if your own hands are very warm from wearing gloves, allow a little time for them to cool down – and *vice versa* – to get a reasonably true picture. If the ears are cold all the way down, the horse is cold: if they are warm at the base only, he probably feels slightly chilly. Put your hand under his rug, if worn, on the loins and wait for a few seconds to get a feel of how he is. He should feel cosily warm. Then run your hand down to his belly and check there. Often this area, due to being clipped, does feel chilly, so a longer rug would help in this case.

If the horse is chilly or cold, you have to decide, within your personal circumstances, what to do about it. He could need more shelter, more food, more clothing, drying out or all four. Even with a wet, outdoor animal, these areas are the guideline areas and, given time for what heat there is to permeate the winter coat, it should still feel warm under the 'wool'. Push your fingers through the coat and the mud and be patient. If no heat is coming through, obviously the animal is cold. And if he is actually shivering . . . !

It is often said that once you start rugging up a horse or pony at the beginning of winter you have to continue as otherwise he will feel the cold and get a chill. A better guide is whether or not he actually feels cold! We do not wear the same weight of clothing during a mild spell as during a cold one, and horses should not either. The horse should be regularly checked (at least twice a day) and his clothing adjusted accordingly.

It should be remembered that the natural insulation layer of a horse's unclipped coat in winter is flattened by clothing, so removing or greatly reducing the heat-retaining layer. Turn-out clothing is a definite advantage for many horses, particularly finely bred ones, in windy and/or wet conditions, but although stabled horses cannot move around enough to keep really warm, because they are not subject to draughts (or should not be), the cold, still air in their stables is no hardship for them if they are unclipped. Rugging up an unclipped, stabled horse is probably counter-productive; it is said that is takes 2 ins (5 cms) of artificial insulation to replace 1 in (2·5 cm) of the horse's natural insulation. Of course, rugging up the horse will give a sleeker appearance to his coat, if that is required, but the non-working animal would probably be more comfortable without a rug. Again, simply use the checks given above to gauge if he is warm enough.

Similarly, on a cold, still day, unless a horse is clipped fairly extensively or you want to keep him clean, he will probably be more comfortable with no rug. If he is turned out on a positively mild day, he could well be too warm if wearing a turn-out rug.

Once the sole preserve of the racing fraternity, exercise clothing seems to be being used more and more by 'ordinary' horse owners these days. Its advantages are considerable, particularly for working owners who are short of time for drying off horses either before re-rugging in the stable or putting on a turn-out rug for the field.

Exercise clothing comes in various weights of fabric, sometimes double-lined, lightly quilted, waterproof but not permeable, waterproof *and* breatheable or simply a very light rubberised nylon sheet to keep the rain off the horse's quarters.

Breatheable textiles obviously come into their own for such clothing, enabling the horse to work fairly hard without danger of remaining clammy and becoming chilled under an ordinary waterproof sheet. On dry days, a plain woollen exercise sheet can be used. Most of them cover only the back (under or around the saddle), loins and quarters, as these are the areas most subject to cold and where the remaining hair on a partially clipped horse is thickest and so takes longest to dry. It is essential to use the fillet string to prevent the sheet blowing up and frightening the horse.

In absolutely drenching weather, there is nothing wrong in exercising in a stable rug of suitable fabric and allowing it to cover the shoulders as well if you are going to be in a hurry on return to the stable and will not have time to thatch and subsequently check the horse. Because the fabric is permeable, the sweat will rise up through it from the shoulders and breast (which sweat most) and if you follow the usual rule of walking the last mile home (or less if the weather is cold) the horse will be dry and fairly cool under the rug, so you can put on his normal rugs.

7 Care of the Feet and Legs

Horses, whether feral and living in wild conditions or domesticated and making themselves useful to mankind for a living, depend for their survival entirely on having four sound feet and legs. The horse's anatomy is that of a super-specialised running machine, having evolved to go on one toe (equivalent to the tip of our middle finger), and at times bearing not only his weight but the multiplying force of speed and maybe carrying a rider too. Driving horses have the stress not of a rider's weight but of a vehicle which has to be hauled over varying terrain. It is not surprising, considering that horses were meant to do none of these things, that the cause of most working horses being out of work is lameness.

The feet themselves normally have a very good blood supply which nourishes the sensitive tissues inside (which bond the bones to the outer horny casing) and carries away the waste, toxic products of metabolism. The main bone of the foot which gives it its shape is the pedal bone and this is the one which becomes partially or even completely detached in laminitis. Tucked in behind that is the navicular bone. The short pastern bone articulates with the top of the pedal bone, and the long pastern bone with the short. The long cannon bone articulates with the long pastern bone and forms the fetlock joint. The two little sesamoid bones come behind the joint, attached by ligaments to the cannon and long pastern bones. Above the cannon are the various small bones which make up the knee and hock, equivalent to our wrist and heel respectively, and with them articulate the radius and ulna of the forearm and the tibia of the thigh.

The muscles mainly involved in locomotion are situated in the forearm, shoulder, thigh and quarters; there are no actual muscles in the lower legs but a complicated arrrangement of ligaments and tendons binding the bones together and attaching to them so that the muscles from which they lead can move the bones by contracting and exerting a pull on the tendon which then obviously moves the bone.

Within the foot, tendons and ligaments are attached and the structure is surrounded by sensitive tissues (the laminae) which bind with the horny, insensitive laminae inside the hoof wall. The wall grows down from the coronary band as our nail grows from our cuticle, and the sole and frog we see on the ground surface of the hoof have their sensitive counterparts inside the foot. At the back of the foot are the heels and, inside, the plantar cushion.

When weight is put on the foot, the whole foot squashes slightly down and out, compressing the blood vessels and so squeezing the blood out of them and on up the leg. When weight is taken off the foot, fresh blood fills the vessels from the leg, so regular blood exchange takes place.

The foot expands most, if only slightly, at the heels, which action absorbs concussion at source, the remaining force being passed on up the leg, diminishing as it is absorbed and lessened by the joints and other structures. In the unshod horse, the frog acts as a non-slip pad to give him security during movement, but in a shod horse, particularly one newly shod, it cannot perform this function as, due to the thickness of the shoe, it is not in contact with the ground on a hard, flat surface (although it can act, if minimally, in softer ground).

The balanced, well-conformed foot and leg pass force up the limb so that is is evenly distributed and no structure is unevenly stressed. When limbs are not straight, when feet are out of balance or when ground conditions are rough resulting in uneven pressure on foot and leg, the forces transmitted are also uneven so some structures, or parts of them, receive more force and stress than they are really capable of taking without risk of injury.

In winter, peculiar conditions such as slippery ice or holding mud can increase the muscular effort needed for the horse to stay upright or to move his legs efficiently, and this can cause muscle, tendon and ligament injuries, particularly if that work is taking place at a fast pace. With shod horses, ice balled up in the feet can cause bruised soles and make even walking difficult and dangerous as the horse loses his ability to 'grip' the ground.

Shoeing horses is a matter of preference or necessity. Resting, outdoor horses in snowy conditions would certainly be better off without shoes as snow cannot become so impacted in the smaller space available within the undulations or unevennesses of the ground surface of a horse's foot. On the other hand, if the horses are out on hard, frozen ground, shoes can prevent cracked, chipped hooves, as on hard ground in summer.

In natural conditions, horses' feet wear down more or less at the right rate for the terrain they are moving over. The foot grows continually and makes up the wear. The quality of the horn depends on diet, but the body also responds to demands made on it by producing harder or softer horn according to the stresses put on the feet by hard or soft ground.

In domesticated conditions, unless horses are working on fairly soft, or smooth, hard surfaces such as tarmac or even moderately on concrete (but not gritted roads), shoes will be needed to prevent excess wear. Then, of course, the shoes prevent any wear at all and the farrier has to remove the excess growth of horn and trim the feet into as balanced a conformation as he can, depending on the natural state of the feet, before putting the part-worn shoe back or fitting new ones.

In winter conditions, there is a great deal your farrier can do to help your horse work safely and securely. Because, in Britain, we are generally more plagued by mud than snow and ice, the traditional fullered, concaved hunter shoe, or its modern derivative with tapered heels fitted with stud holes rather than with specially forged calkins and wedges, is normally best. The fullering offers increased ground-holding qualities and the concaving reduces suction in mud. The pencilled heels also help to reduce suction and the chance of the shoes being trodden on and pulled off by the wearer or a neighbouring horse.

The type of studs you need, if any, can only be decided by your local conditions or those of areas you visit. For road work there are special 'needle' studs, small blunt spikes which just give that extra hold on possibly icy conditions or black ice patches. There are large pointed studs for slippery mud, big square ones for holding mud and, indeed, many different patterns of stud which your farrier should be happy to discuss with you.

I feel that more use could be made in Britain of frost nails. These are just ordinary horseshoe nails with a little blob of hardened material on the head, which offer that necessary resistance to slipping and sliding. These nails, and similar ones with specially roughened heads, are used on the continent and in northern countries such as Canada and Sweden, for racing and polo playing on ice and are most helpful when you cannot turn out your horse but simply have to ride or drive in order to get him exercised at all. In the days when essential personnel such as doctors and delivery firms had to make their horses earn their livings, frost nails were very common.

It has to be admitted that if used for a long period (months) at a time, they can shorten a horse's action slightly, but only temporarily.

Other methods of offering better road-holding are for the farrier to weld into the fullering at intervals (say, toe and heels, or quarters) hardener which wears rough rather than smooth, obviating the need in all but exceptional conditions for studs.

There are special hoof pads which have a slippery surface and which can be fitted between shoe and sole to help prevent snow building up in the feet, also stiff, spongy pads which, because they move under pressure, claim to serve the same purpose, but smearing the soles and frog with old cooking fat, candle wax, ski wax, neatsfoot oil or any other greasy, slippery substance, is just as effective and cheaper, if more temporary.

As at any time of year, the state of the shoes must be checked daily, and certainly before work. Mud can loosen apparently tight shoes and suck off loose ones, possibly tearing the horn in the process.

Constantly wet conditions can certainly have a softening, weakening effect on hoof horn, resulting in worn heels and frogs where they touch the ground, and, in the case of the frog, opening the way for thrush which does not need dirty bedding but simply wet, airless conditions, to thrive. If hooves do become softened, it can be difficult to nail and keep shoes on and the horn is more easily damaged. It does depend on the individual animal, and some live out in wet, squelching, muddy paddocks all winter with apparently no noticeably bad effect on their feet. Others' feet become spongy, in extreme cases, and problems then arise.

There are any number of proprietary hoof dressings on the market with varying claims as to their actions. It is worth discussing with your farrier the properties of any particular brand. In summer, those containing lanolin or glycerine may be beneficial for improving dry, brittle horn, but in winter a dressing which prevents excessive absorption of water would obviously be better. Many hoof dressings are simply oils which sit on the surface of the horn and would help this condition, but much moisture is absorbed through the ground surface of the wall, even when the horse is shod. Hoof varnishes have the effect of sealing the hoof and are disliked by some veterinary surgeons, but in a case of excessively wet conditions and moist, softened horn they could be useful, used under the supervision of vet or farrier.

The obvious answer, of course, is to bring the horse into dry conditions until the problem rights itself, if at all possible.

Continual exposure to salt used on roads in winter can cause or exacerbate chapped skin on the lower legs, and on the belly if the salt-containing moisture during a thaw splashes up. However, having been born and brought up by the sea and having ridden on the beach most of my life on my own and other people's horses, I have never seen horses who work on the beach and in the sea have any problems at all with their feet or legs from the salt. I have no explanation for it but can only say that those animals who have shown themselves to be susceptible to salt should be treated like those susceptible to mud fever, and have protective dressings applied before going out.

Sand itself is extremely abrasive but does have the advantage that it brushes off easily. However, it can cause trouble if horses are exercised in boots. The sand can find its way down between the boot and the leg, the constant movement of the leg creating friction between the leg and the boot, and one very sore leg can be the result. The problem is lessened if bandages over gamgee tissue are used instead, or if gamgee tissue is used under the boots.

Fresh, loose snow has little effect on feet and legs, but frozen, crusty snow can cut skin like a razor. If it is essential to work horses in such conditions, their legs should be protected with exercise bandages applied not too tightly, and right down over the fetlock like stable bandages. Even so, the heels and coronets can become badly scratched. Over-reach boots are not the full answer as the snow builds up between them and the foot. It is obviously better to avoid such conditions if at all possible.

Horses turned out in such snow should be watched for injuries to the lower legs, and treated accordingly. In deep snow, out-wintered horses tend to create paths of least resistance for themselves between shelter, food and water points and follow tracks in the snow which flatten down.

Many owners will naturally want to protect their horses' legs from the effects of salt on the roads and also mud, with its attendant risk of mud fever in some horses. Vaseline is often recommended for these purposes but is only really practical to use on the heels and up the backs of pasterns as it is really too thick to rub through hair effectively. A better preventative, which can be used all over the lower legs, is medicinal liquid paraffin. This is a bland oily liquid which protects against the wet and coats the skin, helping to prevent bacteria getting a hold.

Arguments vary as to whether or not long leg hair really does help to protect the legs against wet and mud. Certainly, ponies which stand in muddy paddocks with leg hair left on are usually free from the disease, although their white socks are sometimes affected. Generally speaking, if your horse has shown a susceptibility in the past to mud fever and chapped skin in general, it is probably better to turn him out for freedom and exercise (but not to make him live out) and, if he grows long, thick leg hair, to clip this off with the coarse blades of the clipper. When he comes in, thoroughly rinse off the mud and dry the legs properly with towels and a hairdryer, and bandage if necessary. Once they are quite dry, apply liquid paraffin to lubricate the skin. If the horse has a fine coat, clipping the legs may not be necessary. When he goes out again, apply more liquid paraffin first to guard against outside conditions. Always pay particular attention to heels and pasterns.

Because liquid paraffin has an oily base, you will probably need to use a mild or gentle medicated soap to break down the oil and remove it. Never use harsh soaps or perfumed ones, which can seriously dry the skin and sometimes cause a skin reaction as well.

The traditional advice for preventing mud fever is to let mud dry on the legs, bandaging over it first, then to brush it off when dry. It is argued that washing mud off rubs it further into the skin, which it irritates and inflames, making it easier for the bacteria to enter. Some owners do swear by this method, but others know from experience that it can, in fact, often actually cause the condition it claims to prevent.

I feel the reason is probably that, as it is the mud which causes favouring conditions for mud fever to develop by scratching the skin, surrounding it with moisture and excluding air, surely it is better to remove it as quickly as possible, so that it spends as little time in contact with the skin as is necessary, and further, that it is removed by a method (hosing or perhaps rinsing off with a watering can without the rose on the end) which specifically does not rub the mud grains against the skin, causing irritation.

Certainly, nothing is more calculated to make the skin sore than dandying or hand-picking off dried mud, particularly hard clay, especially after it has been in contact with the leg under bandages and has been rubbed against the skin with every movement the horse makes.

Of course, even after rinsing off the mud, if you do not then thoroughly dry the legs, particularly the heels and up the backs of the pasterns, the skin may well become chapped and sore; so many owners come unstuck on this simple point of common sense. Once the skin is dry, apply, even if only to the most susceptible areas (heels and pasterns), either liquid paraffin, a mildly antiseptic udder cream from the vet, or E.45 cream from Boots chemists. If the whole leg is likely to become infected, apply liquid paraffin up the whole of the lower leg, rubbing it well in against the lie of the hair to make sure it is really on the skin. Proflavin cream mixed with liquid paraffin makes a good antiseptic preventative oil.

The skin *must* be clean and dry first, otherwise whatever you do apply will simply 'seal' in existing bacteria and exclude air, thus providing ideal conditions for them to spread.

Protective boots of various sorts abound and are always a good idea with young horses or when lungeing any horse. Many owners use them in the field, too, although it is a moot point whether putting them on to protect against kicks and knocks when larking about the paddock can cause another problem in that mud getting inside the boots can rub and cause sore skin. Certainly, if you expect icy patches during exercise, brushing boots and knee pads are advisable, and maybe over-reach boots too.

Winter is the time when yearling racehorses are being tested to see if they are going to be fast enough to run in their two-year-old season and the combination of youth and strenuous work on immature bones and soft tissues brings special problems of its own. Their trainers have to feed for growth as well as work and even slight over-feeding can result in inflamed joints and leg deformities. A little too much work causes concussion and the animals are thrown out of work at a time of year when it may be difficult to turn them out for the exercise and freedom they need to mature physically and mentally.

With any horse or pony, particularly those working and those turned out, a thorough daily inspection of feet and legs is a great help in revealing problems in their early stages so that remedial action can be taken before the problem takes a firm hold. Epiphysitis (inflamed joints) in youngsters can be put right by correcting the diet, concussion by resting the horse and then working only on softish ground, and mud fever can be treated on a first aid basis (see Chapter 10) if caught early, although if the infection gets into the bloodstream (causing serious illness in extreme cases), it is a case for antibiotic treatment under veterinary supervision.

The animals most at risk from skin and hoof problems during winter are white-legged ones, particularly well-bred animals with Thoroughbred and Arab blood. This is not to say that all such animals are going to have trouble, but they are the most likely candidates. By managing each horse according to his constitution and susceptibilities, as in every aspect of horse management at all times of year, problems can be lessened and the horse can remain healthy and useful.

8 Bedding

One of the reasons for providing horses with beds is to keep them warm and protect them from floor draughts, and this is obviously particularly important in winter. Draughts create a chill factor and definitely make horses (as well as humans) feel considerably colder than in still air of the same temperature. Other reasons are to make the floor more comfortable for the horse, to keep him cleaner by draining away or absorbing urine, to encourage him to lie down and rest (so conserving his energy for work and keeping warm!) – and perhaps to provide manure for your roses.

A really good bed may look over-generous to some people, but skimping too much on bedding, at least as regards quantity and quality, is a false economy, because a warm horse eats less, and bedding of any kind is certainly cheaper than food. The warmest bedding materials are straw and paper, the coldest peat, with shavings and sawdust coming somewhere in between. Straw and paper may be more expensive than shavings but the difference is made up by the extra warmth. Of course, the bedding materials themselves do not generate heat; the warmth comes from their ability to conserve the heat coming from the horse's body into the surrounding environment which, when the horse lies down, is obviously the floor. Straw and paper are both poor conductors of heat, so keep the body warmth around the horse better than shavings and sawdust, and certainly better than peat.

Years ago, I saw some very impressive advertisements for peat as horse bedding and bought a few bales to try. Maybe I am fanatically fussy about beds, which I like deep, dry and clean, but I could not cope with the peat at all. It was the super-absorbent type, sphagnum moss peat, as opposed to the more soil-like sedge peat. I found that I could not keep a reasonably dry bed, the material was cold (even having a thin top layer of frost on cold mornings) and I could feel the dust in the air and in my horse's coat, despite a well-ventilated stable. All in all, I could not recommend peat as a bedding, especially in winter. The other beddings can all be suitable, according to your circumstances.

The benefits of keeping a decent bed down in the field shelter should also not be overlooked. Anything which helps to conserve body heat in out-wintered horses, or those out for long days while their owners are working, is worth doing. Horses' number one priority for a place to lie down is that it should be dry, not necessarily soft, and very few fields are dry during a British winter. If the shelter is kept bedded down, apart from being dry (most outdoor horses stay outside the shelter rather than in it), which will encourage the horses to use it, it will also help to keep them that bit warmer.

The three main systems of bedding management are full mucking out, deep litter and semi-deep litter. In the first, the stable is fully cleared of all droppings and wet bedding every day (droppings usually being skipped out several times a day), half-dirty material used as a base for the new bed and new material laid on top and banked up around the sides, partly to create extra warmth and partly to help to keep the horse away from the wall when he lies down, so reducing the chances of his getting cast.

Many people, when mucking out, leave a bare space just behind the door with a view to preventing bedding being 'walked' out of the stable when the horse comes out. The practice may achieve this quite satisfactorily but, particularly in winter, there is a good reason why it is not really a good idea from the point of view of the horse's well-being and comfort, if not the appearance of the yard – and the former is the most important.

Leaving bedding behind the door, right up to it in a continua-
tion of the banking, if slightly lower, ensures as far as possible
that no draughts can come under the door to make the horse feel
cold. Also, this space is where a stabled horse will stand looking
out much of the time. I feel sure it must be more pleasant for
him to have bedding to stand on than a bare floor. Also, if the
feet and heels are wet from exercise and have not been dried off,
bedding will help to do this.

In deep litter, only droppings are removed, the remainder of
the bedding staying in and having new material (and plenty of it
at first) laid on top to consolidate into a thick, springy, warm
and, strange as it may seem at first, dry bed.

With semi-deep litter, which is a useful system for those
working during the week, the droppings and very worst of the
bedding are usually taken out, new material scraped in from the
banking to fill the gaps, and fresh brought in to re-bank.

Full mucking out is suitable for straw bedding and, with
some trouble, shavings. Semi-deep litter is recommended for
paper, shavings and sawdust, but is also good for straw, and
deep litter works best with straw and, perhaps surprisingly,
sawdust.

The ventilation of the stable is always important, but particularly so in semi-deep-litter and deep-litter systems, for obvious
reasons. Drainage is also important, and although little urine
may be seen actually to drain outside a box bedded on anything
but straw (or even straw if it is very broken up due to combin-
ing), putting in large quantities to soak up the pool of urine
which settles in a badly drained box is *not* good management!
The drainage must be rectified, either by having new flooring
laid or drainage channels created in the existing flooring, if
possible, before any bedding system will be a success.

Some floorings drain away urine without actually needing an
underground drainage system installed, with proper drains
(although this can be done, if desired), but before going to the
trouble of having one of these put in, it would be wise to check
with your local council (Department of Public Health and
Safety) to see if they have any regulations. Although such

systems work very well, particularly in areas where the land is well-drained itself and the water table low, people who do not understand horses and may even be antagonistic towards them are likely to look askance at your suggested flooring. The distance your stables are from your living accommodation can also make a difference, according to your local council's particular requirements. If they are far enough away, there may be no need for an elaborate, expensive drainage system and a free-draining flooring can be put in.

The most common of these is loose weave-asphalt laid over (usually) fine gravel, on top of clinker and rubble. The urine then drains through all these substances into the earth, never to be seen again, and your bedding will remain much drier than you would expect. Do tell whoever is laying the asphalt to resist the temptation to ram or tamp it down afterwards (apart from a gentle smoothing off) as this will obviously compact it, fill in the holes and prevent the urine draining away.

Another system is to use old bricks laid on gravel with about half an inch (1 cm) between them. Again, the urine drains through the gaps and the bedding stays fairly dry.

Both these materials are warmer than concrete, which is a cold, hard flooring (but cheap and familiar, hence its popularity). It absorbs urine and does not dry out at all easily.

A flooring system which not only saves a great deal of bedding (it works best with long shredded paper), drains urine right away from the bedding and even provides a layer of insulating air between it and the flooring beneath is the Ridry stable flooring system. It consists of perforated tough plastic tiles which interlock into a platform which is laid on to the existing floor. The bedding is laid on top of the tiles and remains so dry that 'phenomenal' savings in bedding are reported by users. Also, of course, the bedding being dry, the horses lie down readily, and labour is saved, too. (The Ridry stable flooring system is marketed by Janet Cross from Cobbacombe Farm, Huntsham, Tiverton, Devon.) Straw can also be used with the system, but obviously not shavings, sawdust or peat, which simply block up the holes.

The type of bedding material you can use will depend on several factors: its availability in your region, whether or not your horse has any allergy problems which might preclude your using straw, the cost and whether or not you can dispose fairly easily of the resulting manure.

The ideal aim is for most people to sell the manure, which brings cash into their equestrian budget. Straw is usually readily saleable as it is almost universally popular with nurseries and mushroom farms. Shavings is not so popular because it takes nitrogen out of soil, but some firms do take it as it is so popular with horse owners due to the fairly economical cost. The same applies to sawdust. Peat (unfortunately!) is fairly popular and saleable as it is excellent for most gardens, and shredded paper does (equally unfortunately) present problems in its disposal in many areas, although some distributors produce detailed instructions for making highly desirable manure out of it. An acquaintance of mine uses paper exclusively for the twenty-odd horses in his yard and has enviably cheap heating all winter in his home because he has installed one of those 'burn-anything' boilers which burns up the used paper from the stables.

He uses a system of mucking out which I have recommended for years. He mucks out into two piles, one almost entirely droppings and one almost entirely used bedding. When doing each box, he goes along the line with a large barrow removing just the droppings from each box and dumps the load on to a heap in the usual way. Then the worst and wettest of the bedding is removed and put on another heap. Because of its nature it dries out somewhat in the heap and is soon ready for burning in his central heating boiler.

The bedding in the boxes is managed on semi-deep litter, as recommended by the manufacturers and the Animal Health Trust, as I understand it, so the slightly dirty bedding is tossed to air and dry out while the horses are at exercise, then relaid, with fresh on top in the usual way, ready for them to come back in to.

This system would also work just as well with any other bedding material. The resulting droppings pile of manure would be much more saleable than any other manure, obviously, and the bedding pile, particularly if shavings or straw, can be put to good use in winter around the premises.

Shavings and straw can be used to fill up outdoor manèges or indoor schools, cattle yards if you are a farmer, or laid in badly poached areas in the paddocks, such as in gateways, in the entrance to shelters, around watering points and on well-used tracks. It can be laid down to provide exercise tracks in frosty, snowy weather – a most useful function – and may even be sold on again afterwards, depending on your local conditions.

The droppings pile of manure can be sold quite profitably in many areas, particularly where there is a residential population of gardeners or allotment enthusiasts, or market gardens. You could either sell it by contract to a commercial firm or bag it into plastic sacks, such as those in which bedding or hayage are delivered, or old fertilizer sacks, and sell it at the gate. Do not forget to add to this pile the droppings you may pick up from the paddock and field shelter, so increasing your revenue. It does not have to be well rotted, although some purchasers may prefer it so. In that case, simply form three piles, one in the making, one rotting and one ready for sale.

Apart from increasing your horse's warmth and comfort with good bedding practices, remember that badly managed beds encourage respiratory problems, which are common enough in winter due to confinement and possible lack of turning-out facilities, without exacerbating them further with ammonia fumes given off by decomposing organic matter, particularly urine. Standing in droppings or on filthy bedding encourages rotted horn and thrush, and the generally putrid atmosphere in a badly managed stable irritates mucous membranes which allows infections to become established, for instance in the eyes and lungs. Horses who have to lie on dirty bedding frequently develop skin irritations, too.

Take advantage of the money-saving qualities of a well-managed bed and muck system – and keep your horse well and comfortably warm at the same time.

9 Exercise and Work

The provision of adequate exercise is crucial to the health of horses and ponies yet is one commodity domesticated animals very often go short of, particularly in winter when paddocks may be so wet that to turn horses out on them would ruin them for the next grazing season. There are ways round any problem, even if the ultimate solution is not ideal, provided those involved want to solve it badly enough. With a little thought, a willingness to use one's imagination and to adapt, exercise and work need not be so difficult as at first thought.

In natural conditions horses were, of course, free to move at will over many square miles/kilometres of country and even to walk while eating. Only a comparatively few feral herds of horses now enjoy this lifestyle in our over-crowded world; those turned out in domestic paddocks in most countries experience a remnant of that sort of lifestyle. Even in small paddocks (say, under about five acres/two hectares), many horses feel cramped, although almost any turnout facility is better than nothing, in other words being confined to a stable most of the day.

Under normal circumstances, that is in a healthy, sound horse, exercise is needed for the mere maintenance of good basic health and has various closely linked effects on the body.

Its gross effect is that it speeds up the whole metabolism of the body – heart rate and respiration increase, resulting in quicker blood flow and distribution to the body tissues of food and oxygen, and the quicker removal of waste products, which are produced all the time but more so during exercise and work.

Exercise reduces the amount of water and fat in and around the muscle tissues and promotes the development of new muscle cells. The digestive system is stimulated by movement, resulting in more efficient digestion and excretion. The body temperature increases slightly and the skin becomes more active, more supple and more efficient.

Exercise in gradually increasing duration and severity is also the way to bring a horse to fitness for strenuous work of any kind, and the psychological effects of being on the move as nature intended are very considerable. Horses were even meant to move while they eat, perhaps one reason why so many of them either kick or move from one foreleg to another while eating.

Exercise can either be given in the form of freedom in a paddock, corral or yard of some kind or take place under saddle or between the shafts. In the latter case, although the horse probably enjoys being out and about and on the move, he is not free but constrained by the discipline of human dominance, however tenuous. There is nothing he would enjoy quite so much as the freedom to kick up his heels somewhere with plenty of space to do it, to have a good roll without fear of bumping into the stable walls, get up and have a good shake, a buck and a gallop round afterwards. If facilities can possibly be arranged for it, exercise of this kind can be just as beneficial in its way as 'work' exercise and can save owners, particularly working owners, much time at a difficult time of year.

Horses suffering from shortage of exercise become tense, anxious and restless mentally because of the deprivation of natural movement and space around them. Physically, their health is less good because of the slower rate of the metabolism. Food is not digested so well, nor toxins removed so efficiently from the bloodstream, both of which have a deleterious effect on their general well-being. Muscles lose tone so the horse becomes physically weaker, and the combined effect of these factors is that he also becomes more prone to disease and disorders of various kinds. The mental frustration can result in various stable vices as well.

One of the most important connections in horse management is feeding in relation to exercise or actual work done. The horse is *very* prone to serious and most unpleasant disorders resulting from over-feeding, among them azoturia, lymphangitis, colic and laminitis, plus various skin irritations and mental 'lurgies' such as going crackers when he does get out and trying to get rid of the excess energy when he does not, by such means as performing stable vices or simply looking for what we might call mischief – throwing feed and water containers about, prising off loose kicking boards, digging up bedding, nibbling and biting anything he should not and generally trying to relieve his frustration. Horses who behave crazily when out are a danger to themselves, their handlers and anyone nearby, and those who try to relieve pent-up energy when in can equally damage themselves and their stables and related equipment. Depending on temperament, some become bad-tempered in the stable and more or less dangerous to handle. This can spark off a vicious circle of punishment, resulting in soured temper, resulting in more punishment and ill-feeling on the part of handlers, and so on, when all the time the initial fault was not the horse's at all but that of his human connections for not managing him correctly.

If a horse's exercise has to be curtailed for any reason, either illness injury or very severe weather, the first thing that should be done is a very hefty cut in concentrates. Should the horse actually be stable-bound, most animals would be better off with all concentrates cut out except for a single handful in each feed just to keep the digestive bugs going. The short or manger feeds can be as described in Chapter 4 – mainly chop, roots and some grass meal. The most important thing, however, is to give the horse a twenty-four-hour-a-day supply of roughage to keep him both contentedly full without excess nutrients and also entertained, which is most important for a cooped-up horse. The roughage can be clean hay of not too high an energy grade, such as meadow hay, and it is also beneficial to hang up a net of clean oat or barley straw, too, so the horse can have a change of roughage if he wants. If you normally feed a hayage product, switch to a lower energy grade while the confinement lasts, so that you can feed enough to keep the horse full and occupied, as these products are normally consumed fairly quickly and in smaller amounts for the energy provided than is the case with hay.

Unless the horse is feeling ill, do give him a thorough, stimulating grooming every day and, if the weather is mild, let him stand in lighter clothing, or none at all, to give him a break from clothing. Wisping a horse not only stimulates the skin but helps to keep some tone in the muscles during idle periods. 'A room with a view' helps to keep horses interested in the world. They should certainly be able to see each other and what is going on round about them, and most horses appreciate being able to chat to their next door neighbours through spaces of some sort in the boxes, such as grilles in the wall. Their actual doors, however, should be placed so that they cannot get at each other while standing looking out as some timid animals will refuse to look out if they are frightened of an aggressive neighbour. In any case, it is better to remove the neighbour in such a case.

Horse toys may sound silly but many highly respectable yards use them. A tough plastic football on the floor has provided hours of entertainment for horses. It could also be hung up in a haynet for the horse to push at. Large plastic bottles can be suspended at head height in a back corner of the box, and half a car tyre has served well for the same purpose.

Music should be used with discrimination – some horses love it and others hate it, so watch the horses in your yard to find out just how they feel about it. Horses seem to have quite eclectic tastes when it comes to music, anyway. They invariably, in my experience, prefer soothing classical or romantic music to heavy rock or jazz. They also seem to prefer instrumental music to the vocalised sort – maybe they hear enough human voices as it is!

Obviously, extra-special attention must be paid to the cleanliness of the bedding in confined horses. Extra skipping-out should be done and a good bed left down all the time.

From a diet point of view, it is probably easier to get a horse fit in winter than at any other time. Given reasonable ground conditions, they can be turned out to get themselves half fit and keep themselves in shape without the dangers of getting too fat on spring and summer grass, and the rest of their diet can therefore be strictly controlled. While actually working, more of their work can be done at a steady trot, when that stage of the fitness programme is reached, than normal, because the horse will have done a good deal of walking in the field.

Two or more animals in a field together will keep each other on the move, particularly if they are well-fed and not too cold (perhaps being rugged up and having access to shelter), so will stay in a half-fit condition without your having to do the extra fittening work involved. When ground conditions are not fit for work on the roads or tracks, good old-fashioned manure rings may have to be laid down to keep the horses in some kind of work, not only to try and get them fit but to provide the basic exercise they must have to stay healthy or to maintain whatever fitness you have been able to achieve so far.

Spring, at least early spring, presents the same sort of conditions as winter; it is when the grass starts to come through that trouble can start if horses are out, or suddenly turned out after a winter of confinement. If they are being made fit, spring grass must be strictly controlled. If they have had no grass to speak of all winter, begin by grazing in hand for just ten minutes a day, and extend to half an hour by the end of a week or ten days. After this, they can be turned out for an hour or more, depending on the exact conditon of the grass, the horses' individual response to it (whether they easily put on weight or not) and, of course, the weather. It can still be very changeable in spring and horses can get a chill when we might least expect it.

Exercise facilities and opportunities vary from district to district and on whether or not the horse owner has transport to travel to suitable facilities. Racehorse trainers are not the only ones to box to the nearest beach during a freeze.

Most fitness programmes begin with slow walking on the roads and tracks in the immediate vicinity, whether the horse is ridden or driven. It is a definite advantage to have driving horses broken to saddle so that at least part of their exercise can be given under saddle, since this is often quicker and more convenient than putting the horse to each time.

Bridleways are, of course, public rights of way just as much as the road outside your house, and it is a great shame that not all horse owners join their local bridleways groups and become active members. They are ideal places to exercise horses away from the hazards of traffic and to give faster work which cannot be given on roads or on the verges alongside them. In winter, however, they can become impossibly muddy. More damage is done to them by farm machinery and cattle than by horses, in my experience, but even so it is diplomatic not to use them to excess in wet weather. When the ground freezes, the ruts become rock hard, and then they are, of course, dangerous. Joining a bridleways group not only helps to keep bridleways and similar rights of way open and new ones sometimes created, but it also shows the local councils that their maintenance is a necessary job and they *are* very much wanted and needed. If this can be shown to be the case, there is much more chance of their being surfaced properly and kept viable for farmers, riders and other countryside users.

Often, depending on your relations with local landowners and farm tenants, permission can be gained to ride over private land and tracks. This should obviously never be done without permission, and whatever instructions are given regarding exactly which fields and tracks may be used should be followed to the letter. Private land can provide a most valuable extra facility at a difficult time, so it must be used responsibly, as with bridleways.

You may not have your own indoor school, prepared gallop or outdoor manège, but may well be able to borrow or hire such facilities, maybe with a group of friends to share the cost and transport expenses.

If you live within reasonable reach of the beach, again, sharing transport costs to get there, if it is not within hacking distance, is often well worthwhile, as the beach is rideable in all but the most severe frost and heavy snow. You have to check the tide times with the local town hall of the area you intend visiting and remember that it is not only high tide which matters but that the beach will probably be under water for about two hours either side of high tide, so time your visit accordingly. It is normally best to work on the beach *after* high tide, if possible, rather than before, as the sand will have more give in it. It you are intending to do fast work, remember that some beaches, especially those with a crown, pack down solid and are often as hard as a road when dry. If you ride on them just after the tide has gone out they are safer, but still remember that sand, unlike turf, has no spring in it at all. Check also with the local council if there are any very soft patches on their beach, or even quicksands, and avoid those parts.

There are, of course, various ways to exercise your horse without actually riding or driving him. Lungeing and long-reining can be carried out for about half an hour, which, particularly for lungeing, is quite long enough if boredom is to be prevented. Loose schooling could be made more use of with a little modification of facilities. You do not need your own specially prepared jumping lane, but if you have an indoor or outdoor schooling area with a good fence all round, you can still manage.

The horse should first be obedient on the lunge and willing to answer the voice. If you have, say, half a dozen helpers strategically placed to keep the horse out at the fence, you can do without an inner fence, or simply erect one on electric fence-type insulating posts but using bright orange plastic tape instead. A wide variety of jumps can be erected inside your lane and the horses will probably enjoy the freedom and exercise for a change. Of course, you do not have to have jumps or a lane. You might find yourself working out your own circus-style liberty act instead!

Mechanical horse walkers are becoming a more and more familiar device in Britain, and one (from Conveyors International Ltd) has recently come on to the British market which runs on an overhead track in an indoor school, which can take up to twenty-five horses walking or trotting round the track of the school rather than round a central pivot. Another (made by Equitus) is especially useful for those short of space as it can be installed in an outdoor schooling area but its arms fold up out of the way when not in use.

Riding one horse and leading another is a very common way to exercise polo ponies, and some hunt stables also use the method. It does mean you can exercise two animals in the time it normally takes to exercise one. If you are using public, traffic-laden roads, it is not advisable to lead more than one horse, and that one should always be on your left, with you on the ridden horse between it and the traffic. Always lead in a bridle, never an ordinary headcollar, and keep the led horse's head by your knee. Hold his reins with *both* of your hands, tying a knot in the buckle end so there is less chance of them being pulled through your hands. The knot should therefore be on the outside of your right hand with your left hand also holding his reins. It is dangerous to lead the unmounted horse with just your left hand.

Obviously, the technique of riding and leading must be practised at home before venturing out, to make sure both horses involved will take to it. They should both be obedient to the voice and traffic-proof.

Leading a horse on foot is, of course, quite possible, but, although better than nothing, a very restrictive way of exercising a horse in winter. You should always lead in a bridle, or properly fitted lungeing cavesson with the leadrope clipped to the front ring, so you have more control in an emergency. Again, wear gloves and knot the end of the lead rope. Keep to the left of the road on the horse's right and do not lead the horse on the pavement as it is unlawful. Try to find routes where there are convenient gateways to 'escape' into should traffic appear overpowering. Wear strong shoes or boots and your hard hat. Carry a long schooling whip in your right hand to use behind your back for extra control, if needed.

As discussed, turning your horse out is an excellent way of exercising him if, for any reason, you cannot exercise him yourself. Even on frozen ground, horses used to being turned out as part of their daily routine will not go crazy and injure themselves, particularly if you turn them out a little tired and hungry and give them a good hay supply in the field. I find that it is horses who are rarely, if ever, turned out who go mad when given a taste of freedom, so it is to your own and your horse's advantage to make sure he is turned out regularly.

Horses also love frolicking in snow unless it is deep, when it can disguise uneven going and dips in the ground, cause a mis-step and a resultant muscle or tendon injury. Remember to grease their feet well to help to prevent snow balling up in their feet, and pick out the feet before leading them back to their boxes on hard going, otherwise the packed snow could either cause a bruised sole or, should one 'pack' fall out, the resultant uneven gait could panic the horse and cause more trouble.

If there are any icy paths, or patches such as frozen-over waterlogged areas in your paddock, spread sand, ashes or fine grit on them first to help to prevent the horses slipping on them. If the long-range weather forecast has given warning of a freeze set to last, get the winter field rolled to get rid of divots and general rough ground, then when the freeze comes it will freeze level. You can spread old bedding over the most used areas, if you wish, to soften things up a bit, but generally horses are much more sensible about hard going than we think. Turning them out on frozen, rough ground, however, is asking for trouble as they can easily miss their footing, stumble or fall, with disastrous consequences.

Horses can also be turned free in indoor schools or outdoor manèges for an hour or so, just to stretch their legs and add to their exercise quota. Large covered yards are, of course, an absolute boon. They can be deeply strawed or floored with any of the usual materials used for flooring schools and manèges – wood chips of various sorts, probably with a combination of sand, peat and salt, are the most common material. Rubber strips are also available and seem very good, and experiments are at present under way to find a suitable all-weather surface for racehorse gallops with a view to all-weather racing. The options at present are a combination of specially coated sand grains and fibrous materials, and doubtless others will be tried and become available to the horse world in general, as usually happens with bloodstock research.

What if your yard has no suitable turn-out facilities, no indoor school or outdoor manège and fields either so waterlogged or so rough and frozen that it would risk the horse's life and limb to turn him out? Apart from the manure ring or track, why not reassess the premises with a view to providing *some* sort of exercise area, even if it amounts to little more than a playpen? Most yards have the odd area or corner which could be put to good use with a little imagination, surfacing and fencing.

Perhaps there is an area which is always hopelessly waterlogged. Consider excavating out the top soil, selling it and laying bricks (flat) or even rubble, topped by coarse gravel, then fine gravel and maybe (but not necessarily) some sort of wood or tan product for surfacing, or just the used bedding from your stables. The fencing, provided it is high enough, could simply be one top rail on posts, or even electric fencing, preferably the sort with bright, shiny tape rather than wire so the horses can see it better. This sort of facility is perfectly all right for turning out horses for an hour or so, maybe twice a day, to have a canter around and a buck in freedom. If you can make it roughly twenty metres square, you could even use it for limited riding.

I know two people who have done this with previously useless corners of their yards. One, because she sold the top soil from a boggy patch, actually made a profit out of the scheme because the work was done by family and friends.

Wherever you put your horse to exercise himself, make sure he cannot get at frozen ponds, streams or rivers. Horses often walk on the frozen surface and either slip or go through the ice, often with fatal results. They either die from exhaustion trying to get out again, drown or become hypothermic. Such danger spots, including ditches and dykes, should be fenced off.

Ice also takes us by surprise when out hacking. The roads may seem perfectly all right, then a patch looms up in front of us, or, worse still, black ice, often shown up by a bluish tinge on the road, is present. If you cannot avoid the patch but find yourself already on it, give your horse his head, take your feet out of the stirrups in case of a fall and sit still so as not to upset his balance in any way. He will pick his way unless he is unusually stupid, and more often than not you will negotiate it safely. Do not dismount; four feet are enough to worry about. If you are driving, you should walk, obviously, and, again, not interfere with your horse's mouth.

Basic precautions to take when driving in frosty, icy conditions are, firstly, do not. If you are already out and get caught on an icy patch, do not make the mistake of turning your horses in the direction of a skid as you would with a car. A car is a rigid body, a horse or horses and vehicle are not, and you could find the carriage skidding round while the horses are going on. You are liable to smash into trees or whatever is in your path.

If you use the lightest carriage you can (so you do not end up being pushed by its weight, particularly downhill), make certain your horses are well shod with frost nails, have their hooves packed with grease, soft soap or wax and use a breeching, you simply have to trust and rely on them to stop you. Four-wheel brakes are safest and most useful in such conditions but are usually only found on competition vehicles. Whatever you do, do not use your brakes hard, as if the wheels lock you will make matters worse and could cause a very serious accident. Brake very gingerly, if at all.

Most working owners who exercise during the week have to do so in dusk or dark conditions whether they like it or not. With care, this can be just about as safe as riding on roads at any time can be. Choose the best-lit roads you can but not main roads, particularly at rush-hour times. Suburban estates are often ideal. You will not be able to see where you are going on unlit roads and bridlepaths, and although horses do see much better than humans in the dark, it would take an unusually strong trust on the part of the rider/whip to press on into the black unknown!

Reflective clothing for horse and rider is strongly recommended and lights are essential. Vehicles must, by law, have lights fitted, but a horse and rider are not breaking the law by going out without lights, crazy though it may seem. It is, however, the height of irresponsibility to do so. There are plenty of different stirrup lights available from saddlers and the British Horse Society for a very few pounds and they could easily save your life, that of your horse or pony and of other road users who may be caught up in any accident you cause due to not being clearly seen. Cycling shops also sell a good range of lights in the form of cross-belts and wrist lights, so your hand signals can be clearly seen.

Remember that motorists driving along will have their attention focussed at about the level of your horse's hocks, so the type of light which fits to your upper arm is not the best. Get one which clips under your right stirrup and protrudes a little, and get into the habit of putting your right leg out to the side a little whenever you hear an engine coming up behind you so that the light can be clearly seen (red to the rear, white to the front) and is not hidden by your horse's belly from behind – a common complaint from motorists. Have a schooling whip in your right hand for extra control

In addition to lights, wear the palest clothing you can and also a reflective tabard and hat cover, with reflective strips on your horse's legs and bridle. There are also reflective exercise sheets available.

When leading horses to and from fields in the dark, try to have an assistant to walk behind and just to one side of you, carrying a lantern in his or her right hand to warn motorists. Always keep well to the left. If 'in convoy', have people at front and rear with lights. If helpers are not available, wear a light yourself (such as one of the cyclists' battery-operated cross-belts) or make a rough harness out of binder twine and hang motorists' lanterns (white to the front and amber to the rear usually) from the harness on your front and back. It may sound silly, but you cannot take too much trouble where road safety is concerned. Have the palest horse at the rear and the next palest at the front. Lead in bridles for better control.

After any freeze there always comes a thaw, ready to trap the unwary into thinking all is back to normal and work can be resumed without a thought for slipping. Nothing could be further from the truth, of course. The ground underneath the top inch or so will still be frozen solid and lethally slippery.

The answer is to carry on as if everywhere were still fully frozen up. Keep to your frost nails and studs, your manure ring and your roadwork rather than start fast work on the land, unless you have an all-weather facility at hand. Roads which have been badly compacted with frozen icy snow during the freeze can now become even more dangerous as the ice turns to slippery slush, possibly with more ice still underneath, so such roads and lanes are best avoided for a while longer.

When the thaw does finally come properly, remember that your horse may be prone to azoturia if you have not cut down his concentrates sufficiently while on restricted exercise. This will not become apparent until you attempt to resume 'proper' work – even active schooling at working trot can cause problems in some horses, particularly those who have had azoturia before – so build up slowly as if getting fit again.

Horses can retain fitness for about two weeks on restricted exercise, so physically, your horse may be still capable of the work you want to give, but it is still advisable to build up over a few days. If the horse has been on little or no work for longer than that, fitness will have to be restored before he can work in safety.

If you have been able to take advantage of riding in indoor conditions, perhaps by attending indoor shows in the evenings or at weekends, you will have been made aware, if you were not already, of the slightly different riding techniques needed for riding in a comparatively small space. Horses usually become more alert and 'bouncy' indoors, more contained, and find they have to concentrate as the fences reach them quicker. (A different bit may give more control in a cramped arena.) Make full use of the arena, use the corners well, otherwise you are depriving yourself of available space. Give your horse a little time to get used to the lights and crowds if you have been circling around in the dark outside, and allow longer for riding in in cold weather. Even if you have been able to practise in another indoor ring, the atmosphere in the main arena will be different and the horse needs a little while to accustom himself to it. The experience will do him good, and even if you do not normally wish to compete in such events, they do provide a valuable school and exercise facility in adverse weather conditions.

A freeze may mean you have to give your horse a mid-winter rest even when you did not intend to do so, but during a long winter season, possibly living under artificial conditions, a couple of weeks off can really refresh a horse in winter work who might otherwise have become jaded, bored or bad-tempered by late winter.

Gradually reducing the concentrates and the work and finding somewhere to turn the horse free for several hours a day, with a hay supply, is all the let-down needed in winter. Make good use of your New Zealand rug to avoid chills. When the two weeks are up, it will only take a week or so to return the horse to normal work and diet, and he will be rested and refreshed after his little break.

When letting down and roughing off horses in winter or early spring after a season's work, many people run into trouble because they rush the process and try to acclimatise the horse far too quickly. A stabled, clipped, corn-fed horse is a cosseted animal, unable to fend for itself immediately in the open, even when well fed. The letting down and roughing off process must be almost as gradual, at this time of year, as the fitness programme at the beginning of the season. Three weeks is not too long, and then only if the weather is mild and there are no set-backs.

Start by leaving open the horse's top door all the time, if this has not already been done. At the same time, increase the hay but reduce his concentrates by about half to a quarter and reduce the speed and severity, but not the duration, of his work. Stop body-brushing, too, to allow some build-up of grease in the coat.

Next, leave off one underblanket and start turning the horse out for about an hour a day, wearing a New Zealand rug, if this has not been done already. If the weather continues mild and the horse appears all right (not cold or starting to lose weight), decrease the concentrates further and increase the hay/ roughage portion of his diet. Decrease work and increase the time spent out. Continue like this until the horse can be out all day, probably with a New Zealand rug on, and probably with a rug indoors at night.

Then, during a particularly mild spell in spring, leave him out all night with the New Zealand rug on and the same concentrate ration as previously, to compensate for the loss of his stable at night. Keep a sharp eye on his condition and behaviour. If he looks tucked up, his coat is staring, if he stands about looking miserable (which he probably will anyway if he has no companion) or hangs around the gate looking hopefully to be brought in, you should take things more slowly with him. It will not do him any good to be allowed to become actually cold as opposed to slightly chilly, and will not acclimatise him. It will simply take him back in condition and subject him to all the usual ill-effects of a chill.

Keep bringing him in at night, if necessary, with a good bed and haynet. Under the New Zealand rug put another clip-in under-blanket, and let him take his time, according to the weather, if you want to avoid a thin, possibly sick and suffering horse. Obviously, a good shelter in the field will considerably assist the process.

There are two categories of horse which may need special care in winter as regards exercise. They are the old and the young.

Old stagers have seen it all before, and may think they can cope as they did all their lives. They do, however, just like many old people, become more susceptible to the weather as they grow older and feel the cold more. Old horses are better off exercised lightly nearly every day rather than being worked for longer more erratically. Half an hour seven days a week is better than an hour and a half three times a week.

They should not be given a more extensive clip than is absolutely necessary and should be exercised in clothing. If the latter is a new venture for them they must be accustomed to it in the normal way, by being led, tacked up, round the yard, then ridden round and, if all seems calm and orderly (no bucking or playing up), taken out as normal.

If they have turn-out facilities, a warm turn-out rug of some kind should be put on; again, they should be accustomed to surcingles and/or leg straps if they have not been in the habit of wearing outdoor clothing. Their skin, getting thinner and less resilient with age, may be more subject to rubs, so one of the lightweight rugs should be chosen and a careful watch kept for signs of rubbing.

If older horses appear to be losing weight, attention should be paid to their teeth, even if these are normally checked regularly, as there may be sharp edges or hooks present which are preventing efficient chewing and, therefore, digestion of the food. Softer food may be needed, too, to enable them to masticate thoroughly and prepare the food properly for digestion. Check them particularly for feeling cold as this is especially dangerous in older horses. Turning them out for exercise in two shorter spells a day is better than allowing them to become thoroughly cold in one longer period.

Young horses, especially flat-racers who will be barely two years old during their first winter in work, also need special consideration. Work on hard ground, as in summer, must be avoided with young bones and feet. Exercise clothing would probably be appreciated and, particularly remembering their youth, somewhere, maybe on a prepared surface, to have a play every day should be provided. Playing is something all horses do all their lives, but the facilities for allowing it are particularly important for the young, if often overlooked. A horse does not mature until it is 5, sometimes 6, years old. Even then, it is the equivalent only of a young adult human of about 17 to 20 years old – still quite an inclination for play!

10 Health and Condition

Today, we are more able to ensure our horses' health, most of the time at any rate, than at any other, due to advances over the last twenty, and particularly the last ten years in equine research and veterinary knowledge. Certain aspects still outwit us, for instance the control of virus diseases, and in other areas old chestnuts are being squashed as research proves the effectiveness of different ideas and methods from those traditionally embraced. In others still, such as fitness and the management of the sports horse, research is going on at such a rate that it can be difficult to keep up with the latest practices which enable us to work our horses in fitter condition and with less risk to them, provided we apply the principles correctly, than ever before.

But all the research, theories and new practices in the world will do little good if we do not understand the basics of what constitutes good general health in a horse, and are unfamiliar with the disorders he is most likely to come across.

A horse in good general health, not necessarily hard and fit for work, will show an interest in life in general, be alert and have a good appetite for good-quality food. Horses who eat bad food, droppings, excessive amounts of dirt, wood and other undesirable substances, normally have some digestive disorder. The coat should be glossy and smooth; even in winter if the horse is living out the coat should not feel harsh and rough but have a bright appearance through the mud! The skin should be supple and easily slid along under the flat of your hand. The mucous membranes (inside eyelids, nostrils and gums) should be a healthy salmon-pink colour and not reddish, blueish, pale or yellowish.

Droppings should amount to roughly eight piles a day. In a stabled horse fed mainly roughage and concentrates, they should be a khaki colour and of such a consistency that they just crumble on hitting the ground. In a grass-fed horse they will be greener and looser, but diarrhoea or constipation (hard, dry, small pellets or insufficient amount) is obviously a sign of disorder.

The normal average temperature of the horse is roughly 38 °C (100 °F), although this will be slightly higher in youngsters and ponies and lower in old horses, and mature athletically fit horses over 14·2 hands high. The normal average pulse/heart rate is about 36 to 42 beats per minute and respiration roughly 8 to 14 breaths per minute. Obviously, after exercise these rates will be higher, but if they do not start to come down significantly within ten minutes, you could have a problem in the form of overwork or exhaustion. If work is not the cause of high or low rates of all three, the horse is probably sickening for or actually suffering from some disease and the veterinary surgeon should be called.

Stabled horses sometimes cough for about ten minutes on leaving their stables to clear their airways after being in an artificial atmosphere, but if the coughing continues for longer than this, stop work and return home, and give the vet a ring.

In behaviour, horses are normally social animals and, even allowing for herd position – bosses and underlings – stay reasonably close together. They have a personal space which they often like to keep around them, about three or four yards/ metres, but they often go into other horses' personal space for purposes of mutual grooming, fly defence in summer and shared bodily warmth in winter. Any horse which is habitually apart from other horses, standing doing nothing much or picking at its food, perhaps with head down and not sharing in exercise and games, is probably ill and should have veterinary attention. If a horse lies down for more than thirty minutes, this, too, could be a bad sign. This is particularly the case if it is lying flat out on its side rather than propped up on its breastbone with its legs curled around it to one side.

Sunken eyes, discoloured mucous membranes, a hangdog look, dull, rough coat, staring coat, listlessness and a general look of dejection are other signs of disorder which can help us to assess when our horse is not in good health.

Fit horses often undergo a change in temperament. Sweet-natured ones may become less so, nasty ones even more so! A fit and well horse sometimes becomes, as might be expected, full of the joys of spring, but many, particularly when they are overworked and fed too many concentrates, and especially when they are allowed no grazing or freedom, frequently become sour-tempered. Although it may be 'normal' for horses in those conditions, it is a situation to be avoided if we want a contented horse who is, therefore, more likely to thrive and be both physically and mentally able to do the work we ask.

If a horse is feeling cold he will often shiver, just as we do. His skin and muscles may take on a tight look and feel and he will shelter behind even the straggliest hedge or bush, or hang around near the gate, which he associates with being taken in. If his temperature is below normal, he could well be suffering from hypothermia. In this case, he may not even shiver at all, he may show great lethargy and lack of appetite – and this condition can occur on what we may consider a mild day, depending on the length of time the horse has been exposed to the conditions causing it, the availability of food and whether or not other horses are preventing him from using what shelter there is.

The sort of conditions which lower horses most are wind and wet combined with even only a mildly chilly day. They can stand considerable still, dry cold, but are brought down in health and spirits by constantly windy and/or wet weather with nowhere dry to lie down and no way of escaping the weather. Even when they are well fed, this alone is not enough to make up for exposure to bad weather conditions.

If a horse *is* cold, he should be brought into sheltered, dry conditions and rugged up with warm blankets, but direct heat should not be applied. If he is wet, he can be dried off first as described in Chapter 5. A warm feed will have a warming psychological effect on him, and his water should have the chill taken off it so as not to chill the core of his body any further. A generous bed, *ad lib* supply of good hay, protection from draughts and warm clothing are common-sense precautions which will help him to warm up. Obviously, the conditions which brought on his cold state should be avoided in future. Clothing, feeding and shelter are always the prime protectors from cold.

If a horse loses weight during winter it is a sign of over-exposure to chilling conditions and insufficient food. It can be quite difficult to put weight on a horse in winter, particularly one living out, so strict checks should be kept on his condition (bodyweight) from autumn on if this is not done as a matter of course. Also check him visually so you can see whether or not his ribs, hips and backbone are any more or less visible than when the horse is in ideal condition.

The formula given in Chapter 4 can be used, or a special tape purchased, and, with long-coated horses, you can regularly push your fingers through the coat and really assess how much weight they are carrying. With clipped animals, occasional snapshots can be taken during the winter, if you feel this will help you keep track of how your horse should look. Familiarity often blinds us to what is really happening, and a photo or an outside opinion often helps. It is particularly easy to be fooled by a long coat; in cold weather the coat will be 'fluffed up' to trap a thicker layer of insulating air next to the body, and this can easily disguise a thinnish horse underneath if we are relying only on a visual examination.

Stabled horses frequently become tense and fed-up towards the end of a long winter with, perhaps, boring work, no free-dom, a high concentrate ration and insufficient natural contact with other horses. There are, of course, working horses who are never turned out at all, particularly those in many military and police establishments and working delivery horses, but this type of horse often receives much more work, albeit of a slower, balanced nature, than privately owned 'hobby' horses whose work may be insufficient and given in spurts rather than to a proper routine.

A brief let-down of about two weeks, involving a change of work, more relaxation in the form of turning loose with a friend (probably with hind shoes taken off to be on the safe side if the horses are not used to freedom), fewer concentrates and more roughage, more roots in the diet and a generally less urgent atmosphere in their human attendants will usually work wonders in such horses and restore their zest for life and work.

Every horse should have a medical check once a year, even if just a superficial one not involving blood tests, profiles, x-rays or other 'biological' procedures. A more intensive check should be given to horses expected to work hard during the winter, and also after the season has ended so that, in both cases, anything shown up by the check but not apparent in the horse himself can be put right. Old horses should also have a check whether or not they are working so that any insidious changes in their health can be spotted before they become serious and the body's natural defences, because of age, cannot cope so well with them.

Vaccinations usually given in Britain comprise those against tetanus, influenza and rhinopneumonitis. Although there is an effective strangles vaccine, it has not been licensed for use in Britain, to the annoyance of many conscientious horse owners and their veterinary surgeons. Strangles is a distressing respiratory disease most often suffered by younger horses (not particularly in winter), which can leave them with permanently weakened lungs prone to other disorders and with a reduced capacity for physical fitness and subsequent usefulness. Affected horses are often prime candidates for chronic obstructive pulmonary disease (broken wind) later in life. To say that it is not necessary to vaccinate against strangles is ridiculous and the more we press for the vaccine to become available here, the more likely it is to be introduced and more horses saved for an enjoyable and useful life.

When vaccinations are given, it often takes horses a week or two to get over them, so if they are given before the horse's season starts, when he is more likely to come into contact with other horses, ample time should be allowed for him to return to normal. If they are given at the end of the winter, his normal letting-down and resting period will take care of that.

Winter is the time when outdoor horses in particular become infested with lice if they are not kept reasonably clean. Lice live and breed in organic debris such as dandruff, grease and body fluids. They are about 2 mm long and irritate the horse by crawling about on his skin, biting and sucking his body fluids. Horses often rub themselves raw, particularly on the shoulders and neck, and can become anaemic in severe cases.

Louse powder preparations can be purchased from your veterinary surgeon and should be well dusted into the coat twice, at a two-weekly interval. If you worm your horse with a product containing Ivermectin this can kill lice. The drug is capable of killing migrating worm larvae, and is present in the bloodstream and when the lice consume the horse's blood it kills them.

Horses are occasionally, in Britain, infested with sheep ticks which attach themselves by their mouthparts to the horse's chest and belly skin. To remove them, soak a piece of cotton wool in methylated spirit, chloroform or ether so that the tick relaxes its mouth parts and then gently pull it off. If you are in doubt about how to do all this, do get your vet to come along, as if you remove the tick and the mouthparts remain in the skin this can cause a septic sore.

Azoturia is the result of too many concentrates and too little exercise. It is often called Monday Morning Disease (because it occurred in working horses on a Monday after their Sunday rest if their concentrates had not been reduced), 'tying up' or 'set-fast' because that describes the effect on the muscles of the back, loins and quarters. These become rigid and painful and the horse has more or less difficulty in walking. Forced movement can cause muscle damage in severe cases and this is certainly a situation for your vet to deal with. You will feel your horse have difficulty in moving behind and he may begin to stagger. Dismount at once and cover his quarters and loins with your jacket. Do no more than persuade him to walk slowly to the nearest telephone, or back to his box if near home, and ring your vet.

Lymphangitis is another condition related to too much food and too little exercise. Usually only one hind leg is affected; this will appear very swollen and hard, and feel hot. It can also be caused by an infected wound on the leg. The lymph vessels are inflamed and may abscess. This certainly requires veterinary treatment. Cut out concentrates immediately.

Many horses are prone to filled legs which, however, are nothing like as serious as lymphangitis. The condition is caused by congestion of fluid in the lower legs when the horse is standing about for long periods, even if he has had a reasonable exercise quota that day. Such horses can be helped by bandaging the legs or be housed where they can walk gently about, maybe in a pen attached to their box if they cannot be turned out.

Although it is normally better for a horse to be a little better covered with fat in winter, actual obesity should be avoided. If all the warmth-retaining factors such as bedding, clothing and feeding are observed, together with a well-ventilated but draught-free stable and good feeding, it is possible that a good doer might just put on too much weight; in that case a reduction in feeding, probably concentrates, would be in order. Working horses, in particular, should not be allowed to become overfat because of the usual strains of working in a fat condition.

Colic can occur at any time of year but may be more common in winter due to horses being stabled and on a large quantity of dry artificial (grain) food. The usual signs of colic should be watched for – patchy sweating, the horse looking round anxiously at its flanks, snapping at the flanks, restlessness and maybe getting down, rolling and getting up again *without* shaking, as is normal after rolling. The horse's water intake should be monitored. If he has an automatic drinker, try to use the kind with a meter so that you can see if he is drinking enough. Colic can always be serious so a vet should be called if it is suspected. Opinion these days is against giving any sort of colic drink and against incessant walking around, but check with your own vet on these points. If the horse becomes violent, keep out of the way and wait for the vet.

If a horse is victim to any stable vices already, long months of being stabled are likely to exacerbate them, and actually bring about vices in susceptible animals – those who find being stabled for long periods, plus having to cope with an artificial diet, particularly stressful. More natural management and lessening of stress is the way to prevent all behavioural problems of this type developing. The same sort of regime as mentioned earlier in this chapter should be introduced – more freedom, company, more roughage and fewer concentrates, plus more roots in the diet, and neighbours the horse likes. Action should be taken as soon as a so-called vice is spotted, as once established many of them can become almost impossible to cure.

Probably the most troublesome complaints which occur in stabled horses are respiratory ones. Chronic coughs develop, nose-bleeds become more prevalent, horses become more prone to respiratory infections and COPD is given an excellent chance to take hold. Indeed, many horses who have otherwise clear wind become definitely thick in the wind in winter, even if they develop no other problems, and while management of the COPD horse is relatively easy in warmer weather, it can present real difficulties in winter.

COPD is an allergic condition due not only to fungal spores but to the irritating effects of dust in the atmosphere. The allergic response of coughing and wheezing is due to an over-reaction of the body's immune response which narrows the air passages in the lungs and really does physically make it very difficult for the horse to breathe properly. Working an affected horse can, in bad cases, cause heart failure.

There are various ways to overcome these problems today. Clean-air management is one of the best techniques – proper ventilation should be installed in the box, the bedding should be of paper or dust-extracted shavings, the horse should be removed from the box during and for at least half an hour after mucking out and full deep litter should not be used for such horses due to the build-up of moulds in the decomposing bed.

The box should be regularly swept or vacuumed to clear it of all accumulated dust on ledges, rafters, etc., and the horse should be fed moist food and a hayage product for roughage, or thoroughly soaked hay. Simply sprinkling or even throwing water over it is useless.

Two products new on the market at the time of writing are very helpful in overcoming the effects of almost constant stabling and a possibly resultant stuffy or dusty atmosphere. The first is Stable Boy, described as a stable deodoriser. The distributors' description of it runs: 'It is a totally safe, natural, porous rock granule which has the ability to absorb ammonia and other noxious gases, by a process of ion exchange. It absorbs the moisture and gases of a stable and subsequently allows the water to evaporate back into the atmosphere, but it retains the harmful gases. The product's acceptance and use by major studs, racehorse trainers, competition, show and horse owners in North America is now being emulated by horse owners and trainers here in the United Kingdom.'

The product is spread directly on to the floor of the stable before the bedding is laid. As with any product, the instructions on the pack should be followed for most effective use. It is distributed by Saffron Properties Ltd.

The second product is Dust Cure, a hay- and straw-cleaning machine which thoroughly cleans hay and straw of dust and fungal spores, making them safe to use again even for COPD affected horses, claim the marketing company, Sedgemoor Developments plc.

The machine is fully portable but must be connected by a qualified electrician to a 20-amp single-phase electricity supply. A mains water supply should also be made available for a hose connection to the exhaust of the machine, or it can be collected in a bag. The machine takes in the material, combs and vacuums it and delivers a loose, clean material ready for use.

Your veterinary surgeon can offer treatment for COPD with various drugs both to help dilate the airways and to minimise the allergic response, and many formerly badly affected horses, when put on this combined regime, have returned to normal quite hard work. There is certainly no need to write off a COPD horse these days.

The opposite to being over-stabled is obviously to be turned out all the time exposed to everything the weather has to offer. The most common exposure ailment encountered in winter is undoubtedly mud fever. If a case does get hold, you must act quickly, as if it becomes established it can take months, not weeks, to cure and may get into the system and cause blood poisoning.

Any scabs on the legs must be softened and removed, maybe under a local anaesthetic or at least a sedative from the vet, if they are really painful, which they often are. The bacteria live in the oozing pus and raw skin under the scabs, away from oxygen, so they must be exposed before topical treatments can be applied. Antibiotic ointments are usually used, and in bad cases antibiotic injections will be needed. The horse must obviously be kept in dry conditions, which means a stable with a dry, clean bed. Straw can often prick the legs and be most uncomfortable, so shavings or paper would probably be better.

A related condition, more common in warmish wet weather such as autumn or a mild winter, is rain scald or rain rash. This is caused by the same bacteria and fungi as mud fever but occurs on the upper body, mainly the neck, back, loins and quarters. Similar prevention and treatment apply in this case. At least with rain rash, a light waterproof sheet can be worn to keep the back dry, whereas no one has yet invented Wellington boots for horses! Like mud fever, rain rash can be painful and can put the horse off work for some time, so keep a watch for it and act promptly if it seems to be occuring.

Softened horn and 'worn' heels and frogs can result in certain horses on wet ground, and not always those with white feet. Thrush, an infection of the soft horn of the frog, can take hold in any wet conditions, not just wet, dirty bedding. There is a nasty smelling, dark discharge from the frog, which will be tender when pressed. Sometimes, if the case is quite bad, the horse will 'paddle' from one foot to the other in his discomfort. The infected horn must be pared away and the foot cleaned and dressed daily with antiseptics. The horse must be housed in clean, dry conditions.

Another condition quite common in winter is chapped skin on the face. This is most common in windy conditions and when discharges are not sponged from the face daily – or when they are but the skin is not properly dried afterwards. If infection is present, antiseptic creams should be used after bathing with saline solution. Vaseline petroleum jelly can help to prevent the condition recurring but if it is common in any particular horse it is better to stable him in draught-free conditions than continually to expose him to the wind.

These are the most common disorders which affect horses in winter. As ever, it is advised that any horse owner buys a good, *up-to-date* veterinary book and keeps it handy after studying it thoroughly, and is not hesitant to at least ring the veterinary surgeon to check on any doubtful points. Trying to economise unreasonably on veterinary fees can simply result in more expense later if whatever condition is present fails to respond to first aid. Also, giving the wrong sort of first aid can make matters worse and complicate treatment for the veterinary surgeon when he or she is finally called in.

11 Winter Pursuits and Activities

One great thing about horse sports is that there is something to do all year round. Although certain sports within the horse world do have seasons, such as eventing and long-distance riding, the preparation for them involves activity at most times of year and there are plenty of equestrian activities to take part in during the winter – bearing in mind that your horse will want a rest at *some* point!

Hunting is the most obvious activity in winter, apart from hunter 'chasing, steeplechasing and hurdling, which are professional sports for which amateurs need a licence, not to mention a suitable, high-class horse and plenty of courage. Almost everyone can hunt, from tiny children to frail senior citizens. You do not have to follow the field but can take easy routes round if you know the country or are accompanied by someone who does. Most areas of the country are covered by at least one pack, and there are foxhound packs and harriers in many districts.

For those who object to hunting proper, there are drag hunts where hounds follow a specially laid trail and hunt a human 'quarry'. Drag hunts, however, often involve larger, stiffer fences requiring better riding and a more competent horse if you wish to follow the line, and have none of the unpredictability of other types of hunting. They do, however, provide a good sporting outlet for those who hunt to ride rather than the other way about.

Indoor show jumping now has a very competitive circuit all winter. Once something of a curiosity, it now attracts serious amateurs and professionals alike competing in all grades. It is particularly useful for young horses being brought on. This does not mean that there is no room for novice or 'fun' riders. There is a class to suit everyone and such shows are a good way of keeping your horse in meaningful work during the winter even if you do not show jump during the summer.

Indoor shows of all kinds now abound during the winter, from showing classes and dressage competitions to combined training (dressage and show jumping combined) and gymkhanas for children. Pony and Riding Clubs hold indoor meetings of various kinds, including instructional classes, and most large riding centres with indoor schools hold evening instruction classes at which private owners with their own horses are often welcome.

During the latter half of winter, eventers and endurance/long-distance horses and ponies will be being prepared for their spring season, ground conditions permitting. Many riders say, however, that it is normally easier to get a horse fit during the winter than during summer, when the ground can be baked hard during a dry spell.

Autumn and spring are the times for hunter trials, too. Less formal affairs than eventing, they do, however, have regional and national championships for the really competitively minded, and they are an excellent, indeed probably essential, adjunct to the training of event horses. Some hunter trials do not have an optimum time for their completion, the first home with the fewest faults being the winner, which has led to far too fast speeds in some cases. The better ones, however, set a maximum and minimum time speed, like eventing. Though cross-country courses, unlike eventing, hunter trials often contain such obstacles as gates which have to be opened and sliprails which have to be taken down and replaced, and are, therefore, much more like hunting from which they stem.

Team chasing and point-to-point racing are two more sports which also stem from hunting.

In team chasing, you compete in teams of four and a reasonably well-matched team is important as the object of the game is that you all stay together. Many horses will go well in team chases as they have the psychological support of other horses and do not have to jump in cold blood. Again, there are all levels, but generally, you need quite a high-class horse to be successful at the higher levels.

It is said that the point-to-point course is where you find those on the way up and those on the way down – meaning up-and-coming 'chasers and those who feel it is time to take things a bit easier. However, many point-to-pointers are neither; their owners simply love point-to-pointing, with its fairly short spring season, finding the time demands less than steeplechasing and the amateur, if very competitive, atmosphere quite adequate for what they want. Point-to-pointers do, of course, have to hunt to qualify, but few of them are seen out with hounds after Christmas as their training intensifies and the start of their season draws near.

Two sports never, to my knowledge, seen in Britain are skijöring and sleigh riding. We do usually have some snow during the winter, but our winters do not usually freeze so hard or provide enough of the dry, powdery snow favoured for these two sports.

In skijöring, the horses are often Thoroughbred and you are pulled along on skis (obviously) so need to be a competent skier yourself. This sport is popular in Switzerland, Scandinavia, Canada and in parts of America.

Sleigh riding always conjures up pictures of Christmas and jingle bells, passengers well muffled up in blankets on normally open sleighs going home to hot punch and muffins. It is very enjoyable and exhilarating and used to be popular in Britain up to Victorian times. Due to our apparently milder winters, it has not enjoyed anything like the revival of carriage driving as a sport or hobby.

While some horses are working hard all winter, others are resting, but without the advantage of idle days in the paddock with the warm sun on their backs. Out in the paddock they may be, but when the warm sun comes round they will be working with probably little chance to enjoy it. Such horses as resting flat-racers, polo ponies and show horses will be brought back into work around Christmas time, having had several weeks off during autumn and early winter, and by the time they are brought up again, trainers will already have a good idea whether their 'young entry', the yearlings purchased at the various autumn bloodstock sales, are likely to be fast enough to be worth training on for their first season as two-year-olds.

Winter can also be a critical time for weaned foals, many of whom are weaned very suddenly and rather too early, according to nature's rules, in domesticated conditions. Even native-pony weanlings benefit from being brought under cover, maybe in a large barn together, on winter nights. In fact, youngsters often do better when kept in mixed company together rather than being consigned to individual stables or sharing with one other. In such an arrangement, they either suffer from loneliness or, if in pairs, one inevitably becomes the boss and the other has nowhere to escape to. A more natural herd of youngsters, preferably with a 'nanny' mare or gelding, creates less work and makes for better socialised young horses more mentally stable and with better manners than those reared in more conventional but highly artificial ways.

When it comes to handling them, they often seem to learn quicker and have more confidence in themselves and by spring can be well on the way to becoming really well-mannered animals, outgoing and more worldly-wise.

Although it can be a very unpleasant time of year, winter can also be very busy and rewarding. I hope this book has shown that, with reasonable facilities and common sense, any horse can be brought through it in healthy condition, both mentally and physically, a credit to its owner.

Index